Presented To:

_____

From:

_____

Date:

_____

THE
GIFT OF
GIVING

JIM STOVALL & DON GREEN

THE GIFT OF GIVING

LIVING YOUR LEGACY

AN OFFICIAL PUBLICATION OF THE
NAPOLEON HILL FOUNDATION

Published and distributed by:

SOUND WISDOM

P.O. Box 310

Shippensburg, PA 17257-0310

717-530-2122

info@soundwisdom.com

www.soundwisdom.com

Cover/jacket design by Eileen Rockwell

Interior design by Terry Clifton

ISBN 13 TP: 978-1-64095-199-0

ISBN 13 eBook: 978-1-64095-200-3

For Worldwide Distribution, Printed in the U.S.A.

1 2 3 4 5 6 7 8 / 24 23 22 21 20

In loving memory of Florene Finn Stovall,
whose life was a testament to
the wealth that giving brings.

CONTENTS

Part I

THE ULTIMATE GIVING GOAL

1

Chapter 1

TRULY WEALTHY

Remember that your real wealth
can be measured not by what you
have, but by what you are.
—NAPOLEON HILL

stood on the Oral Roberts University chapel stage,
microphone in hand, addressing the student body. My
wife Crystal and I had returned to our alma mater for
a special chapel service in which we were to present the

university with a check for $1 million, a donation that would launch the Stovall Center for Entrepreneurship.

There is something incredibly surreal about revisiting the place you attended college in the capacity of a donor. Being able to partake in the work of the educational institution that taught you what it means to be an engaged citizen—that is real wealth. As Napoleon Hill's quote that opens this chapter reveals, material riches alone are a poor measure of success. More important is how those resources are stewarded as well as how other, less tangible resources like time and talent have been shared. The ability to give back, whether through service, encouragement, or charity, is something that every single person on this earth has, regardless of their financial circumstances.

Hill is known around the world as the expert on amassing wealth, power, and prestige. His 1937 book *Think and Grow Rich* distilled the insight of 500 of America's greatest businesspeople and thought leaders into a manifesto for personal success that inspired a generation to overcome the limitations of the Great Depression and that continues to inspire entrepreneurs and cultural icons today. But what is often missed in conversations about Hill is that although his "Science of Success" is useful for building financial riches, the true aim of his achievement philosophy is creating the emotional and spiritual wealth that comes from living a meaningful existence. Add value to yourself, yes—but do so in order to add value to the lives of others.

For decades, Hill's achievement principles have supported my success journey, which, as you will discover in this book, is not aimed at a bigger paycheck, a more robust investment portfolio, or a larger house. It is, and has always been, a giving journey...a quest to find the cause about which I am most passionate and, following this discovery, aligning my work, life, and income in such a way that would enable me to give generously to this cause. While I gave much thought and planning to amassing financial riches, along the way I stopped calculating my wealth based on the amount of money I had accumulated and started defining my wealth by the things it could do for other people.

As part of the College of Business, the Stovall Center for Entrepreneurship is the culmination of my giving journey, the biggest manifestation of the legacy I endeavor to live. Along with the other visionaries behind this Center, I envisioned it as providing the essential knowledge, skills, and ethics needed to equip ORU students to engage the world's biggest challenges with God's best solutions. It would do so by enabling students with exceptional abilities to create new business concepts, start-up incubators, accelerators, and launchpads. It would also host workshops, boot camps, and lectures; set up networking with entrepreneurial collectives; provide space for entrepreneurial faculty and professionals to mentor and coach students; and allocate resources for mission-based entrepreneurial initiatives such as micro-financing and venture capital.

My wife and I had donated to ORU in the past, providing over 500 scholarships to students over the last 30 years and even earning the honor of having the administrative building named after us, but this endowment to fund the new entrepreneurship center took our giving to another level. It enabled us to establish a sustainable gift, one that helps people help themselves and then help others. As I'll reiterate throughout this book, you do yourself and others a disservice if you merely throw money at them; it's important to set up a system that enables your money to keep supporting others beyond the initial receipt of the funds.

After passing an oversized check written to the amount of $1 million to ORU president Dr. William M. Wilson, Crystal and I returned backstage. Still riding the elation of the moment, I asked her, "How does it feel?" After all, we were $1 million lighter than when we had come in that day, and I was wondering whether excitement about the gift's magnitude was transforming into shock or concern. Crystal had been raised in poverty in a little trailer house that her family rented in Upstate New York, and we were very poor when we first got married.

So I asked her, "How does it feel to be $1 million poorer?"

Without missing a beat, she responded, "I've never felt richer in my life. Giving that money away was the first time I truly felt wealthy."

Crystal was demonstrating the profound satisfaction brought by peace of mind, what Hill describes as "the wealth without which you cannot really be wealthy."[1] As Hill explains in detail in *Grow Rich! with Peace of Mind*, a book written at the end of his life that contains some of his most poignant reflections on what success truly entails, peace of mind refers to much more than material comfort, or what Hill calls "money-success." In fact, in his list of the twelve great riches of life,[2] money occupies the very last position:

1. A positive mental attitude

2. Sound physical health

3. Harmony in human relationships

4. Freedom from all forms of fear

5. The hope of future achievement

6. The capacity for faith

7. A willingness to share one's blessings

8. A labor of love as an occupation

9. An open mind on all subjects

10. Self-discipline in all circumstances

11. The capacity to understand others

12. Sufficient money

"A willingness to share one's blessings" refers directly to generosity of spirit, but many of these riches derive from or inspire charity as well. Money is certainly necessary to provide material security and the occasional luxury to enjoy, but it is not an end in itself. As Hill explains, "Money will buy a great deal but it will not buy peace of mind—it only will help you find peace of mind."[3] Money, then, becomes a vehicle for obtaining a greater form of wealth, for true riches are found in the peace of mind that generosity brings.

"Life-success," as Hill terms it, comes from pursuing a definite purpose, overcoming the ghosts of fear and any external restrictions to chart your own path in life, and adding value to the lives of others. In Hill's words: "Peace of mind helps you live your life on your own terms, in values of your own choosing, so that every day your life grows richer and richer."[4]

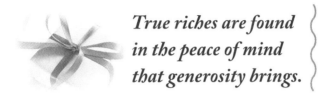

True riches are found in the peace of mind that generosity brings.

Make no mistake: these values require you to be community minded, looking outward to your fellow human beings and determining how you can help them obtain peace of mind as well. For as Hill suggests, "The surest way of finding peace of mind is that which helps the greatest number of others to find it."[5] Giving is foremost a boon to the giver, whose life will be immeasurably enriched through acts of service and charity. My own giving journey reveals the power of continuously dedicating portions of one's time and money to worthy causes, and it is my hope that this book will help you discover this priceless form of wealth so that you can create and enjoy your legacy now.

Now is the time for your ultimate giving journey to begin…

Chapter Two

EMPTYING MY POCKETS

> Life proceeds according to the
> great Law of Compensation. The
> more you give of what you have,
> the more comes back to you—and
> it comes back greatly multiplied.
> —NAPOLEON HILL

This is a story that, had I not been there and lived it, I would not believe it. If I turned this into a script, producers would laugh in my face—it's that unbelievable.

A college football star whose career ended before it even began because of a rare degenerative eye condition, broke and without job prospects, makes a commitment to donate $1 million to a cause to be determined and goes on to found the Narrative Television Network and become the best-selling author of over 40 books, including 8 that have been made into major motion pictures. Who would believe that? But as Napoleon Hill famously said, "Whatever the mind can conceive and believe, it can achieve."[6] That has proven true in my life in the most amazing ways.

Rewind the clock back 40 years—I was sitting in the fourth row from the back of the same chapel in which I was now presenting a check for $1 million. Oral Roberts introduced our guest speaker for the day, a gentleman who was digging wells in Sub-Saharan Africa so that the people there could have clean water. I found it interesting, but to be honest I didn't give it much thought at first.

After the man finished speaking, Oral Roberts said, "I think we should take a collection from the 4,000 of us here today to help this man with his work."

I thought it was a neat idea, except I had only $17 to my name at the time and it was all in my pocket. I had a $10 bill, a $5 bill, and two $1 bills. That was my entire life savings. What was more, I was planning to use it that evening to take a young lady named Crystal out on a date.

Crystal had been one of the students assigned to read me my textbooks, as my vision was progressively worsening during college. I'm not sure she had any thought of or feelings toward me at the time, but I instantly fell in love with her and informed the university that we wouldn't be needing any of the other readers. I decided right then and there that I would either make it through college with her or not at all.

Either you give God your best and expect the best, or you keep your money because you're going to need it.

On the day of that chapel service we were far from a couple yet, so I was hoping to stretch my $17 as far as it could go to impress her. I hesitatingly pulled out a $1 bill, and as the collection basket approached me, Oral Roberts came up on stage and said, "Somebody in this building needs to hear this right now." And then he continued, declaring something that has stuck with me over the years: "Either you give God your best and expect the best, or you keep your money because you're going to need it." I tucked the $1 bill back in my pocket and dropped my $10 bill into the collection basket. It dawned on me then that I was going to have to plan for a $7 date.

After the service, I rejoined Crystal. Hoping my humor would charm her and hide my embarrassment, I told her, "I have some good news and some bad news. The good news is that I helped the man with his wells. The bad news is that we're getting ready to have a $7 date." She, of course, was very gracious about it and said that we could just eat in the dining room on campus and then go for a walk.

While strolling along the campus grounds, we ended up in an empty classroom in the Graduate Center. Sitting across from each other on desks, we talked about our coursework and sundry other things. The conversation turned to our future plans, and Crystal asked me, "What do you think we're going to do when we get out of college?"

It's common to have moments of inspiration, but too often we don't have moments of follow-through.

Mind you, this was the first time she had used the pronoun "we" in the context of the future, so I felt pretty good about our potential. I could still see a little bit, so I jumped up and began writing on the whiteboard: "First, I'm going to start my own business and become a millionaire. Then I'm going to write a book, which

14

will later become a movie. And then I'm going to find something I care about as much as that guy cared about digging those wells, and I'm going to write a check for $1 million for it." I stored this list of goals in the back of my mind. It's common to have moments of inspiration, but too often we don't have moments of follow-through.

Although I didn't know it at the time, that donation to the clean water project in Africa launched me on a personal giving journey—one that would bring me greater returns of prosperity and peace of mind with every contribution of time and money that I made.

Chapter Three

CHARTING A PATH

The starting point of all achievement is DESIRE.
—NAPOLEON HILL

Thanks to Crystal's help, I made it through college. I discovered that I wasn't just a dumb jock and ended up graduating second in our degree program. Crystal graduated first in our program, which was tough on a competitive guy like me. It's okay to be number two, unless you're living with number one. I've developed a theory over the years that maybe she didn't read me all the textbook material. I have no evidence to prove it, but it makes me feel better.

During my senior year, it dawned on me that I would be graduating soon and needed to line up work. As a young man, my greatest aspiration in life was to be a professional football player. The scouts assured me that I had the requisite size and speed; it was just a matter of living until I was making a living playing football on Sundays. I had no safety net, no backup plan. I didn't think I needed one.

Then one day, I went to the doctor for a routine preseason physical and received some very unexpected, unwanted news. It was an extensive physical...you see, they want to make sure you're healthy before they take you out to kill you on the football field. And so they poke you, prod you, weigh you, and measure you—just to make sure you're in prime shape to take a beating. During this visit, however, I had been left alone in the doctor's office for quite a while following the examination, and I thought, *Boy, this physical is sure taking a lot longer than usual.*

Eventually, a doctor came in and shined a light in my eyes. Then another doctor came in, and he also shined a light in my eyes. And then a third doctor came in and performed several other tests. Finally, after what felt like forever, they took me down a long hall, sat me down at a table, and told me something that completely changed my life. They said, "Jim, we're not sure why, and we're not sure when, but we do know that you're going to be totally blind and there's nothing we can do about it."

Your whole world just stops right there. My short and sweet research into the matter informed me that there had never been a blind player in the NFL, nor has there been one to this day. You know, anyone who has seen some of the recent preseason games might question that, but I'm assured that no blind guys have ever made it. It just doesn't happen. I had no idea what I was going to do.

My father got out of the Navy in 1955 and took a job at Oral Roberts University in my hometown of Tulsa, Oklahoma. As a young man, I had sworn that the last place on God's green earth I would ever go would be ORU. I mean, it was just impossible to me. But I'm fairly convinced that the Almighty is endowed with an incredible sense of humor. Any time we say we'll never do something, we might as well pack our bags right then and there.

Lo and behold, because it was too late for me to get in anywhere else, I agreed to go to ORU that fall. I shifted my athletic career to become an Olympic-style weightlifting champion, but until my senior year I hadn't considered how that would translate into a job and a means of reaching all those goals I had mapped out on the whiteboard.

So, I decided to attend a career fair on campus. A bunch of recruiters were there, and my friends were receiving job offers right and left. But nobody seemed interested in offering a blind jock a position. I realized that I was going to be out of college soon...and unemployed.

My father was still working at ORU as the chief financial officer. He had an office in a building right across the street from the campus. I went over to his office feeling dejected and just a bit sorry for myself. I told him the most thrilling thing a parent of a young adult could hear: "Dad, when I graduate in May, I'm not going to get a job."

My dad raised his eyebrows in consternation.

"I'm not going to get a job, but I'm going to start my own company."

He responded, "Come back tomorrow. I'll give you something."

After hearing this, I was thinking, "Alright, the old guy is going to give me $50,000 to help me get started. I'll have a pretty nice cushion to launch my big business."

The next day, I returned to his office early, excited and ready to receive my windfall. My dad was sitting at his desk, and he said, "I told you I was going to give you something. And actually, I'm going to give you two things: First, I'm going to give you the certain knowledge that if you ever earn anything in this world, you got it on your own, because I'm not giving you a dime. And second, since I have no experience as an entrepreneur, I'm going to introduce you to the guy who has the office next to mine: Lee Braxton."

Lee Braxton was a self-made millionaire who had been raised in a low-income area of North Carolina during the Great Depression. With only a third-grade education, he had dropped out of school in order to help support his family. He and his brother opened a bicycle repair shop and diligently saved up a nest egg while paying his family's bills. One day, while working at the store, he and his brother heard a terrible sound. Running across town, they discovered that two freight trains containing small appliances had collided. They chanced upon the insurance adjuster responsible for evaluating the claims and offered to purchase the goods for pennies on the dollar. When World War II began and American manufacturing became focused on supporting the military, Braxton and his brother created a booming business reselling these goods, making millions in the process. Mr. Braxton ended up giving 90 percent of his fortune away and lived off the remainder. Then he went to work for Oral Roberts University for an annual salary of $1 for the rest of his life.

My dad took me into Mr. Braxton's office, introduced us, and then left the room so that we could talk. At the time of our introduction, Mr. Braxton was quite elderly, and I discovered that he was a rather gruff, plainspoken man. After my dad departed, Mr. Braxton asked me pointedly: "Your dad tells me you're going blind. Can you still read?"

"Well," I said, "it's slow and difficult, but I can."

He handed me a thick book, Napoleon Hill's *Think and Grow Rich*, and said, "Read that."

I replied, "Sir, it will take me a lot of time and effort to get through that."

Mr. Braxton responded matter-of-factly, "I'm okay with that."

As he ushered me out the door, I tried to ask him more questions, but he just smiled and gestured toward the book in my hands before finally walking away.

I left his office feeling overwhelmed but hopeful, ready to dig into the dog-eared copy of *Think and Grow Rich* that this business icon felt was so critical for success.

Chapter Four

A SHARED LANGUAGE

The way of success is the way of
continuous pursuit of knowledge.
—NAPOLEON HILL

A week later, I returned to Lee Braxton's office. Getting right down to business, he asked me a number of questions about *Think and Grow Rich*. I was feeling good that I had managed to complete the assigned reading with my limited vision, but when

I answered his questions, my eagerness was quickly checked by his frankness.

"Not the right answer," he would say. "Read it again."

I would come back the following week, and we'd go through the same process—Mr. Braxton asking me to explain the various principles Hill outlines in the book, me formulating what I thought were decent responses, and Mr. Braxton concluding, "Not well explained enough. Read it again."

Mr. Braxton was a proponent of the idea that books could be some of the best mentors available to us. He told me that I eventually would have a team of people supporting my success, but for now the only way I was going to access the wisdom of the mastermind was to read their books. Throughout the years, I've learned firsthand from working with the world's top earners that one of the traits they share in common, especially the self-made millionaires, is that they read many more books than the general public—and Napoleon Hill's *Think and Grow Rich* is one of the most frequently cited as foundational in the lives of top achievers. Mr. Braxton knew there was gold in it, but he encouraged me to find it for myself. Despite my persistent request to know, "How do I get rich?" he would always direct me back to *Think and Grow Rich* and tell me to be patient and diligent in my studies.

I read Hill's book cover to cover three times before I apparently had enough of a correct understanding of it for us to begin our lessons in earnest. Although he assigned me other books to read as well, *Think and Grow Rich* always formed the basis of our conversations. It was our shared language—really, the only thing we had in common. But it built a bridge between our lives and disparate experiences, as it continues to do for so many around the world today.

Hill's notion that "Every adversity has the seed of an equivalent advantage" was particularly impactful at that point in my life, as I was losing my sight.[7] Mr. Braxton taught me that particular Hill quote is the key to success in business, as all an entrepreneur has to do is find a problem and solve it, or find a need and fill it. Hill's concept, paired with Mr. Braxton's insight, eventually led to my idea of the Narrative Television Network, as my blindness became an opportunity for personal success and service, rather than a roadblock or reason for failure.

One of the most important lessons that I learned while under Mr. Braxton's tutelage was the necessity of a giving mindset to one's success in life. As we walked across the college campus, Mr. Braxton would often pause in front of the dormitory that had a sign over the door that read "Braxton Hall." As we stood there, he would say, "If all your goals in your millionaire destination are only about you, it's never enough." This may be a good point for us to consider when it is appropriate to give anonymously and when we accept name recognition. Mr. Braxton had his name on several buildings, and I have followed suit throughout the years. However, he also did many things, as I continue to do, that are anonymous—providing millions of meals for disaster victims, scholarships for families of fallen warriors, and all manner of philanthropy. I believe it is valid to put my name on an act of charity only if doing so makes a difference for the people I'm trying to serve. I want every student who goes to the Stovall Center for Entrepreneurship to realize that once there was a struggling blind student with $7 in his pocket who had a million-dollar dream. In this way, my name creates momentum, motivation, and hope for those young people around the world we are serving.

Mr. Braxton is frequently on my mind, especially lately, as I sit in on meetings preparing for the opening of the Stovall Center of Entrepreneurship. Even though he passed away many years ago, I feel as though he is still with me, sharing in the fruits of my giving journey. For Mr. Braxton, making money was, and should always be, an act of altruism. As he explained, "The best thing you can do for poor people is not be one of them. Not all rich people help poor people, but at least they have the choice, whereas no poor people can help poor people."

I am so thankful that he introduced me to *Think and Grow Rich* and helped me use it to better understand the true meaning of wealth, a discovery that kept my business pursuits focused on finding ways to add value to people's lives. Adding value, as Mr. Braxton taught me, is not only about writing a check. Just as he worked for the university for $1 a year until the end of his life, I have found ways to couple my efforts with my finances as I plan my giving. I do one speech for free for every one where I receive a fee. So one week I may be in an arena talking to many thousands of salespeople or executives, and the next week I may be talking to a few dozen people in a nursing home or a third-grade classroom. I have an office at the Stovall Center for Entrepreneurship where I can offer my experience and expertise to students. Additionally, I use the contacts I have built up throughout my 40-year business career as a resource to introduce aspiring entrepreneurs to people who have already made their mark in the business world. I have millions of books in print and offer my contact information to all of my readers around the world as a way to give back and add value. When you couple your efforts and your time with your financial resources, you can find a giving equation that allows one plus one to equal ten.

When you couple your efforts and your time with your financial resources, you can find a giving equation that allows one plus one to equal ten.

Napoleon Hill's 17 success principles form the universal language of desire and meaning. For all those who want to pursue a cause bigger than themselves or who want to dedicate their life to a driving passion, this book offers the essential building blocks not only to leaving a legacy, but to living one in the present. It was the cannon that propelled me on my personal quest from poverty to prosperity, upon which I elaborate in *The Millionaire Map*. It unlocked the key to success and fulfillment, enabling me to better my own life so that I could better the lives of others.

Not only did *Think and Grow Rich* provide me with lessons on entrepreneurship; it is part of the reason I came into contact with Don Green, the executive director and CEO of the Napoleon Hill Foundation, so many years later.

One day I was listening to a show that Oprah was doing in which she described being at an elaborate book industry event where everyone had high-tech, glitzy booths and displays...with the exception of one guy in the corner who had nothing but a pile of books on his table. She went to explore why this lone gentleman had such a crowd in front of his booth, and she discovered that it was Don Green with a stack of *Think and Grow Rich* books. That book and its message have attracted people seeking success for generations, as it will continue to do in the future. Because of how integral *Think and Grow Rich* was to my own success, I called Don and introduced myself to him.

Hill's message was the cement that bound me together with my mentor, Mr. Braxton, and my dear friend and collaborator, Don Green. One day, Don called me up and said, "Do you realize your mentor, Lee Braxton, was Napoleon Hill's best friend?"

I answered, "No, I had no idea."

He responded, "Yes, he even delivered the eulogy at Hill's funeral. I'll send you a transcript."

Don sent me that transcript, along with a file containing letters that Hill and Braxton had exchanged. And these letters, which will become the basis for a future book, reveal why Hill's message continues to be relevant. As I read the decades' worth of correspondence between Napoleon Hill and Lee Braxton, I can't help but think about what we've lost here in the 21st century in using texts and e-mail to communicate, as opposed to our parents and grandparents, who sat down and created real letters for friends, family, and colleagues. I remember one specific exchange of letters in which Hill was imploring Braxton to come work with him and his partner, W. Clement Stone, on a venture they were launching. Mr. Braxton's reply letter expressed his gratitude for the gracious offer, but he felt he needed to stick to his mission of serving generations of young people from around the world through his work at Oral Roberts University.

Don has contributed greatly to my success and giving journeys in other ways, as well. For many years, I have written a weekly syndicated column that appears in newspapers, magazines, and online publications around the world. Several years ago, thanks to Don, we were able to resurrect and repurpose hundreds of columns that had already been distributed by re-releasing them as a compilation in book form. To date, there have been four volumes of the Wisdom for Winners book series. All of the funds from all of those sales have gone to benefit the Napoleon Hill Foundation and their work at the University of Virginia's College at Wise, where the Foundation has its offices. Hill was a native of Wise, Virginia, and the Foundation continues Hill's work in a very personal way by supporting the community and the college there. Then recently, when my mother passed away, the Foundation redirected the funds from the Wisdom for Winners book sales to the Napoleon Hill Foundation's Florene Finn Stovall Scholarship for Music Students, as a tribute to her and her lifelong passion for music.

I've also been involved in many more of the Foundation's projects. I've had the honor to provide endorsements and commentaries on new publications containing Hill's teachings. I've spoken at Napoleon

Hill Day, the annual commemoration of Hill's birthday, an experience that enabled me to share my time and insight with the student body at UVa Wise. In my keynote speech, I shared Hill's profound influence on my life and the enduring relevance of his achievement principles. Primarily, I spoke on three core messages: first, you have the right to choose; second, you are one quality decision away from anything you want; and third, you change your life when you change your mind.

When your actions are directed toward a chief goal of sharing your talents to add value to others' lives, countless opportunities will come your way. For chances to serve and chances to succeed are one and the same, if you view them rightly. If you focus on giving of yourself now, in whatever ways you can—large or small—you'll discover the true wealth that's inside. And if you share your gifts with enough power, dedication, and persistence, it's unlikely that material success will be far behind.

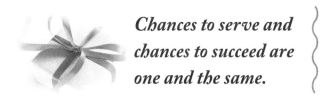

Chances to serve and chances to succeed are one and the same.

The wealthiest and most successful people understand the reciprocal relationship between giving and earning, which is why they rarely focus on money—they focus on the value they can create. After all, the only long-term, consistent way to earn money is to create value in the lives of others. Trying to get rich quick on every venture is a surefire way to become and stay poor. Don't worry about the immediate return. It's more important that you find a pursuit that generates sustainable value. In the long run, you will find that the interest on value compounds mightily. And if you can align your business pursuits with the cause or causes that really motivate you, all the better! When you can combine your philanthropic efforts with your entrepreneurial ventures, you become a world changer.

When you can combine your philanthropic efforts with your entrepreneurial ventures, you become a world changer.

It's this message, inculcated in me by Lee Braxton and Napoleon Hill and reflected in the life of Don Green, that drove my professional and financial success. I have been on a success journey that was always at its core a giving journey, for its motivation was not merely acquiring money and material goods just for the sake of it. Rather, my motivation and my reward—for it is both that which inspires service as well as the fruit that derives from it—has been the peace of mind that results from earning and managing money to better others' lives.

When I began my business career after graduating from ORU, I worked to build a nest egg that could be mobilized, when the opportunity arose, to serve individuals in need. That chance came about when I discovered the lack of accessible television programming for people with visual impairments like myself. The Narrative Television Network that I founded and oversee generates financial wealth, which I can put to work through charitable contributions, but it also creates value in people's lives by enabling them to enjoy educational and entertaining TV content. So while I support and do work for many nonprofit organizations, I also make a true and lasting difference in people's lives when I go to work every day as an entrepreneur. When you understand that you will earn more money if you make a bigger difference in the lives of greater numbers of people, you will discover that becoming financially wealthy is in fact a function of performing great service for other people.

Through my corporate efforts at Narrative Television Network, we have opened the world of movies, television, and educational programming to millions of blind and visually impaired people around the world. The success of NTN has allowed me to become an arena speaker, the author of more than 40 books—8 of which have been turned into feature films—and a columnist whose articles are read globally. These profitable ventures have done as much or more good than many nonprofit organizations or charity efforts.

Once I began to understand the importance of giving, I created a foundation known as the Stovall Fund, which is aligned with other families who have foundations here in my community. Collectively, we can do more than any of us could do individually. We have a staff of people who perform due diligence on any organizations or causes that we want to support. Often, the various family foundations will join together to fulfill a need that none of them could afford to do on their own. But probably the most powerful impact of the group dynamic is the culture of giving that grows around people who are gathered together for the purpose of making a difference in the lives of others. I have long believed that we become like the people with whom we spend the most time. I believe that your income, success, values, beliefs, and priority for giving will all be supported by the people with whom you spend time. Money is an important element, but it is a commodity that can be replaced. Our time and whom we spend it with is what will really make the difference now and in the future.

How do you ensure your business endeavors and your philanthropic actions are aligned as you progress toward your ultimate giving goal? The questions found in "Your Giving Challenge" at the end of the book will help you get and keep these areas of your life productively intertwined, but in essence you should think of all your various pursuits as part of a pyramid—or some other three-dimensional shape if you have more or less than five major pursuits. For the purposes of this example, list the five major ways that you expend your time, talent, and treasure. These should be designated as the corners of your pyramid. For instance, my entrepreneurial ventures focus on books, television, movies, syndicated columns, and speeches. Although I participate in other ventures, my working life revolves around these five pursuits, so they form my pyramid. I like to think of whatever activity in which I am currently engaged as the point of the pyramid, with the other four activities supporting my current focus. But for the shape itself to retain coherence and stability, it is crucial that these five endeavors be directed at a larger goal—a large-scale, enduring way of adding value to people's lives beyond the immediate, short-term effects. My pursuits all align to support people in empowering themselves through entrepreneurial values to empower other people. In this way, success transcends the individual level and becomes a multigenerational, community-wide, and even global legacy that can be enjoyed now and in the future. What sort of value do your ventures all share in creating? If there is not one clear driving purpose, identify the cause about which you're most passionate and work to calibrate your efforts with it.

As you build wealth and influence, the destination you work toward should include many things you want to do for other people and organizations that are important to you—but it should not be just your *destination*; your *journey* should include opportunities for philanthropy as well. After Crystal and I achieved one of our first milestones of financial success, we started a scholarship fund with other ORU alumni that has enabled us to send over 500 young people to college over the past 30 years.

Many years after we launched our scholarship, we had the vision to create the Stovall Center for Entrepreneurship. The university began a global search for an executive director to lead the program. They settled on Dr. Kevin Schneider and asked me my thoughts before they offered him the position. Dr. Schneider's academic and business achievements were stellar, so we agreed to offer him the position. When they introduced Crystal and me to Dr. Schneider backstage before we went out to present the million-dollar check in front of 4,000 students, faculty, and staff, Dr. Schneider was very emotional and exclaimed, "You have changed my life." I let him know that while Crystal and I agreed with the university's decision to hire him as the executive director of the Stovall Center for Entrepreneurship, the decision had been made by the president and the board of the university. Dr. Schneider corrected me, explaining, "No, it's not the position that you've offered me; it's the fact that 20 years ago, when I was an undergraduate student at this university, I was running out of funds and in danger of being forced to discontinue my education when I received a letter from you informing me that I was to receive one of your scholarships. That made it possible for me to get my degree, complete my doctoral studies, and get the life experience necessary to return here to lead the Stovall Center for Entrepreneurship."

Giving becomes an upward spiral of impact and success. You may know what seeds you plant, but you may never fully understand the exponential impact they will have in places and ways you never could have imagined. Having monetary riches means absolutely nothing unless they are put to work to serve you, the people you care about, your community, and the larger world in ways that you find meaningful.

If you have a clear goal and know the value you will generate through achieving that desired end, you will take consistent, deliberate action to achieve it. Hill perhaps put it best when he said, "The more you give, the more comes back to you."[8] The law of reciprocity—this holds the key to the legacy you can live out in the present. What untapped resource will you begin to share with the world right now?

Chapter Five

FINDING WAYS TO SERVE

> Never in the history of the world, has
> there been such abundant opportunity
> as there is now for the person who is
> willing to serve before trying to collect.
> —NAPOLEON HILL

People often view charity as exclusively monetary in nature. However, it is just as important to give of your time as it is to give of your money. How many opportunities to render service have you missed because you didn't think you had enough to offer anyone *yet*? By pushing this responsibility off to some undetermined future date—some imaginary time when you'll suddenly have "enough" free time and extra money—you lose valuable chances to build and enjoy your legacy now, in the present.

When we start out in life, we have a lot of time and little money, so we should be giving a little money and a lot of time. Later in life, the opposite scenario is likely true: you'll give more financially as your salary and savings increase. To be sure, this isn't always the case, and there are plenty of people in retirement living on Social Security checks and carefully budgeted pensions or 401ks who give of their time quite generously. Think of all the retirees who provide complimentary childcare services to their grandchildren or those who volunteer at the local animal rescue, hospital, or community center. People who may not have a sizable financial reservoir in their twilight years often provide invaluable contributions to their communities through these acts of service.

Regardless of your scenario, you should always be giving some money and some time. Those who are blessed with great financial resources should also be giving of their time; it's dismissive just to write a check and be done with the cause. As I mentioned earlier, I give one free speech or presentation for every paid speech that I make. In doing so, I donate my time and, in essence, my money, and the returns are amazing: in addition to the satisfaction I receive from adding value to people's lives, these donated talks enable me to continue to develop and share my gifts and oftentimes attract new opportunities. If you're in the population of high earners, don't discount the value of being generous with your time and money. Doing so might foreclose future opportunities and hold you back from achieving your loftiest goals.

If you're going to succeed in life or in business, the first rule of anything is that it isn't about you.

Those who might be in the early stages of amassing wealth should similarly be sharing both their time and their income with others. This provides two payouts: first, in the enjoyment you will receive from your philanthropy; and second, in the greater success that you will gain from your work ethic. I've had the privilege of meeting a number of billionaire families, who have invited me to speak to their heirs on how to become mindful with their wealth and generous with what they have, and I've learned from their achievements the most crucial success secret there is, one that applies to creating happiness, wealth, or however else you define "success"—and that is simply this:

People who succeed in any area of life intuitively know this, or at least have learned it the hard way and adjusted their actions accordingly. Everyone says, "I want to make money." The only people who *make* money are at the US Mint. The rest of us have to *earn* money, and this can be done only by creating value in the lives of other people. As any basic economics class will teach you, money itself has very little use value. You can't clothe yourself in it to keep yourself warm, you can't eat it for sustenance, and it doesn't function as a tool to build anything. What it has is exchange value: it is only worth the value its adds to others' lives. It's a tool where we store effort. If you want more money, you must generate more effort—give without and beyond the expectation of return. Or in Napoleon Hill's words, "Add value to your work and you set in motion the forces that make the concepts of your mind turn into the realities of living."[9]

So if you're going to succeed in life, you have to quit thinking about yourself. You should wake up every morning and ask yourself, "Whom can I serve, and to whom can I impart value?" Become a giver, not a taker, and you'll be amazed at the positive transformation in your life—personally, relationally, and financially.

The question arises: "What can I share, if not money?"

The word *philanthropy* has as its roots a Greek phrase meaning "loving people." No matter which of your resources you're trying to steward, I encourage you to think back to the original meaning of *philanthropy* and use your gifts to love people. And remember, the best way to love people is to help them better their own lives.

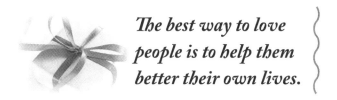

The best way to love people is to help them better their own lives.

If you're looking for some concrete examples, Napoleon Hill offers three ways of sharing that are available to anyone, regardless of their financial situation:

1. Share your special skills or knowledge.

What unique talents, gifts, or expertise do you have? Who would benefit from these special skills or knowledge? What is one way you could translate your gifts into a resource (a donation of time, energy, or money toward a specific end) that you share with a specific recipient or community? Are you a skilled knitter who could make and donate hats for newborns to your local hospital? Are you fluent in another language and could volunteer your time to be a translator? For more help discovering your strengths and talents and aligning them with a purpose or passion, visit the section in the Appendix on "Your Giving Challenge," which will help you turn your hopes and generous inclinations into a concrete, achievable giving plan.

2. *Share by filling a gap when you see one.*

Is there a problem that remains to be solved or an issue that needs to be addressed? Identify this gap, and then create a product or service to fill it. Also attune yourself to gaps that take the form of empty board positions and other opportunities to serve. As Napoleon Hill encourages us to ask, "Who could use your help? How can you help? It doesn't take money...all it takes is ingenuity and a strong desire to be part of genuine service. Helping others to solve their problems will help you solve your own."[10]

3. *Share by recognition and appreciation.*

This gift requires very little effort on your part, but it can make all the difference in the life of the recipient. How many times has your day been completely turned around by a kind word from a boss, co-worker, friend, family member, or even a stranger? You're on the bus heading home from a long day at work, your thoughts lodged in the muck and mire of the stress and demands of your job, and a fellow passenger pays you a little compliment that immediately snaps you back into a positive frame of mind. Or, you're nearing burnout, feeling completely overwhelmed by the tasks piling up, when your boss praises you for a job well done—what felt like an insurmountable to-do list now is something that you power through with energy and enthusiasm. Another example: you're dining out and are tired, hungry, and just a little bit frustrated by how long your meal is taking to arrive. Rather than complain to or about your frazzled server, you encourage him with a word of thanks and praise for the service he is rendering. Not only does your dining experience improve, in terms of both the quality of service and the positive feelings to which you've now tuned your mind, but you've helped your server feel less harried. Give the gift of acknowledging good work, of praising people for their efforts, and of complimenting people for their unique attributes, and you will immediately receive the dividends of a gift that always pays itself forward.

To share a few examples of how these principles have worked in my life: I created the Narrative Television Network after identifying a gap in the way that broadcast media served (or rather, failed to serve) people with vision impairments. I took my passion for equalizing the experience of blind and sighted people, translated it into a business venture that filled a critical gap, and now my company not only generates monetary resources, but, more importantly, it benefits millions of visually impaired people and their families around the world by making movies, television shows, and educational programming accessible to them. With the columns and books that I write, I am able to share the specialized knowledge I have developed over the years as an entrepreneur and someone who has studied success psychology in great depth. These inspire other individuals to doggedly pursue their dreams while also, in many cases, supporting recipients of the Napoleon Hill Foundation's generosity in their educational pursuits. As a way of sharing my appreciation for outstanding service and to recognize great attitudes, I like to surprise hotel housekeepers and restaurant servers with $100 tips. I'm not trying to impress them. Instead, I hope to prove to them that their own worth is far greater than they might have thought.

I never waited until I had "made it" to share these gifts. I found—and, in many cases, created—these opportunities to serve by focusing on my underlying motivation for giving: bettering others' lives through access to uplifting content, educational opportunities, and entrepreneurial values. All of this was directed toward my ultimate giving goal: creating a progressive center for training and developing entrepreneurs who better their own lives, and those of others, through their leadership, and who would create innovative solutions for the demands of the modern world.

The day might never come when you feel like you have "enough" time or money to share it with others, so don't wait for your budget and calendar to be padded. Instead, start finding ways to serve now, this very moment. By seeking out opportunities to give of the resources you have available, you will gain crucial perspective, enjoy more readily the fruits of your labors, and reap more personal and professional success. Start somewhere. Start today!

PRUDENT FINANCIAL MANAGEMENT

Tell me how you use your spare
time, and how you spend your
money, and I will tell you where you
will be in ten years from now.
—NAPOLEON HILL

We tend to think about money only in times of scarcity and abundance, but if we don't think about it, we cannot prioritize appropriately. And if we aren't actively aligning our financial habits with our priorities and values, then we are wasting the most precious resources of all: our time and life energy. Every month we should take time to manage our money, ensuring that it is working as hard for us as we worked for it.

There are only three things you can do with money: spend it, save it, or give it away. With every dollar we have, we should be engaging in each of these activities. A portion of every dollar we earn should be spent on the things we need to sustain us, a portion should be saved and invested for our future, and a portion of every dollar that comes into our hand should be given to people, organizations, and causes that make a difference in the world. These three behaviors are intricately intertwined, and they should be triangulated to achieve the peak of prosperity: your ultimate giving goal, and the peace of mind that results from experiencing your self-discipline, hard work, passion, and talents combine to produce a tangible outcome that betters humanity.

Spending

We all have a budget or spending plan—or a way to make our money go as long as our month does. How we assign purpose to our dollars reveals our priorities. Here's an exercise that will be particularly revelatory: Look back on your spending over the past three months.

Categorize your expenditures, and find out how exactly every dollar was spent. How much money did you spend on clothing that you didn't need and hardly ever wear? How much went to takeout or fast food that could have been cut in half by eating healthier home-cooked meals? After you've assessed your spending, write out your top three spending categories, and reflect on what these categories would say about you and your values to someone who did not know you. Do these perceptions align with how you view yourself? Do they align with your actual values? If not, how might you adjust your spending so that it better reflects your beliefs and goals?

Most Americans fail to reach their financial goals, not because they don't have enough money, but because they don't effectively manage the money they have. There is immeasurable wisdom in the parable of the seed corn, which goes like this: The farmer who consumes his entire crop without saving his seed corn will quickly expend all his resources and will have nothing to generate new resources in the next planting season. On the other hand, the farmer who eats a portion of his crop and saves the seed corn to plant will create for himself a sustainable farming practice, where each year will bring new returns.

The financial application is quite evident: if you spend everything you earn, you'll have nothing to live on. Worse is when you spend everything you earn plus some and are mortgaging your farm and your family's security to enjoy a glut of corn from your neighbor, whose farm is expanding every year at your expense. I'm certainly not saying you can't enjoy nice things, and I don't like to value some purchases over others—everyone should decide what is important to them—but if you're draining your resources in a way that inhibits your ability to save, give, and live securely, you're doing yourself, your loved ones, and the world a disservice. The key is to live prudently, not poorly.

Live prudently, not poorly.

Early on in our marriage, Crystal and I converted my office into a makeshift apartment so that we could save on rent. People thought I just arrived at work early. But we made this choice consciously so that we could direct our limited funds toward something we valued more than an impressive housing situation. We also used to sleep in our ten-year-old Pontiac that we lovingly referred to as The Green Dog when we were on long road trips rather than pay for a hotel. Every time we went to the grocery store, we brought a calculator, and Crystal would add up the cost of each item that went into our cart so that we did not go over whatever amount in cash I currently had in my pocket. We made these decisions consciously so that we could direct our funds to ends that mattered more to us than momentary creature comfort. Although we didn't have $1,000 in our bank account until I was 30 years old, by focusing on how much money we wanted to give away, we never felt impoverished, and we never felt compelled to waste money on trying to impress people.

You know, you can often tell a real millionaire by the *lack* of the trappings of wealth that he or she possesses. Warren Buffett is known for never driving new cars, for living in the same modest home since 1958, and for maintaining the same respectable, but not lavishly decorated, office building for over 50 years. Living by prudent financial principles kept me balanced as I increased my paycheck. I am thankful to have avoided that famous dictum to which so many people fall prey: "We buy things we don't need with money we don't have to impress people we don't like."

What truly matters to you, and is that where your financial resources are going? If not, it's time to reprioritize.

Saving

Saving gives you the peace of mind that comes from avoiding personal debts. But more than avoiding uncertainty and embarrassment, it helps you prioritize. It shows you the true value of money. Napoleon Hill explains how "the habit of saving does away with the habit of waste. As saving becomes a need, through habit, many a man finds he can live just as well as he did before, on the same salary, and this even if some prices have gone up. Why is this? Because he stops throwing away portions of his money on needless or frivolous items; he buys more carefully; he conserves his clothing and other possessions. He finds out how to make his money do its absolute most for him."[11]

Saving money enables you to use it for truly worthwhile purposes, a determination you have the freedom to make through sustained reflection because your financial decisions aren't driven by scarcity or mindless consumerism. When saving becomes a non-negotiable part of your financial plan, you gain strength of mind, which bolsters your success and primes you for doing remarkable things with your time and money.

Savings and investments are a down payment on our future and the future of others. Debt, on the other hand, is a drain on our destiny.

A proper savings plan enables you to create abundance that will benefit your life and the lives of others for the long run. It is the gateway to financial generosity on a grand scale. I like to think of compounding as the Eighth Wonder of the World. If you grow your money through good investments, you're able to multiply the value you can share on an exponential level.

It is amazing how many sizable endowments come from individuals with average salaries. Not too long ago, there was a story in the news about a social worker who died and left $11 million to charity. According to reports, the gentleman, Alan Naiman, was known for his frugality, and he stunned everyone when he passed away and left so much money to various nonprofits in the Seattle area—namely, organizations serving children, veterans, and people with disabilities.[12] Naiman is the perfect example of someone who creates and maintains a savings goal with a clear priority in mind. He dedicated his life to children, leaving a career in banking to become a social worker. In addition, he served as a foster parent and was the caretaker for his brother, who had developmental disabilities. He ensured that he would make an impact in his new field by taking on three different jobs, and rather than spending his income as it came in, he stored the bulk of it away in savings and investments, excited for the day when the receiving organizations would learn of their endowments. According to his friend and the executor of his estate, Shashi Karan, Naiman took great pleasure in thinking about how his money would benefit these groups. Naiman is the perfect example of someone who managed all his resources—his time, his talent, and his money—with great care and consideration. Even though he bequeathed his financial gifts after his death, he lived his legacy every single day by consistently attending to his spending, savings, and giving plans and by dedicating his time and effort to caring for those in need.

As you plan your savings goals, consider how giving might play a role in them. What is the number that you would like to give away to charitable causes—either at the end of your life or annually? Settle on a number, and then structure your monthly savings and investment goals accordingly.

One means of integrating your savings and giving plans is to open a donor-advised fund, which is like a charitable investment account. With a donor-advised fund, you can grow your money tax free, and when you decide on which charities you'd like to contribute to, you can donate money (either cash or long-term appreciated securities) for a tax deduction. It's a great option for planning your legacy in a way that maximizes your giving potential.

To reiterate, saving money is not a practice that should be exclusive to the wealthy; we all should save a portion of every dollar we earn. As Hill affirms, "Anyone can save, and the effort you make toward saving a percentage of your income gives you a true knowledge of the value of money."[13] This insight fosters that invaluable gift of peace of mind and ensures you become a good steward of your financial resources, regardless of how limited they might be.

Giving

The first two types of financial plans—spending and saving plans—are very common. The third type—the giving plan—is less frequently enacted. However, the giving plan might be the most important strategy of all, for it explains how you will direct your monetary resources not exclusively toward consumption or growth, but to adding value to others' lives. It directs your money outward, rather than inward, creating the sort of returns that better humankind.

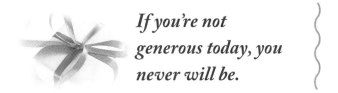

If you're not generous today, you never will be.

Unfortunately, so many people approach giving the wrong way. They say, "Once I'm wealthy, I'll be a giver." No, you won't. If you're not generous today, you never will be. People think they'll get wealthy and then will have extra money with which they can be generous. Those people who are waiting to give are like the guy at the fireplace who says, "Give me some heat" before he gets the firewood. We don't give from *extra* money; we give from every dollar we bring in.

Our capacity to consume is absolutely overwhelming. I know people who make $1 million each month and don't have any "extra" to give. These are the "millionaires" whose net worths likely don't reflect their paycheck and who spend more time trying to look like a millionaire than act like one. But the vast majority of millionaires give away a higher percentage of their net worth and income than the rest of society, and it's not simply because they have more money to give. In reality, these millionaires were givers when they were poor and have continued the habit after becoming financially successful. I would go so far as to say that millionaires don't give because they have money; at least in part, they have money because they give.

As I have the opportunity, in the aftermath of my novel *The Ultimate Gift* and the movie based on it, to meet with billionaire families, I aim not only to change their minds about giving, but to change their habits as well. In this way, I can have a greater impact on the world of philanthropy than just through my own giving. At the Stovall Center for Entrepreneurship, it is my goal over the next 25 years to inspire 1,000 college students from around the world to take on the same giving challenge that Crystal and I did when we were in college. If these young entrepreneurs can visualize themselves giving away $1 million, they will inevitably have successful businesses, personal finances, security, and great lives. If 1,000 of these young people can learn that giving is the key to successful living, their collective efforts and gifts will exceed $1 billion.

Those who have more financial resources to share need to establish a plan for continued giving—a system that will enable them to live a legacy in order to leave a legacy. It's easy to give away money when you're wealthy, but it's harder to set up a structure that ensures the longevity of such charity. Consider the example set by Bill Gates and his wife, Melinda, with their nonprofit that is reported to be the largest private foundation in the world, boasting an endowment of over $50 billion. Mr. Gates is known for saying, "It's harder to give the money away responsibly than it was to earn the money in the first place." He and his wife model how financial generosity should come from a structured giving plan, rather than being a response to a donation request or an isolated effort to offset your taxes.

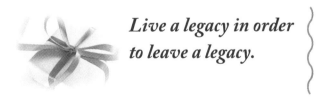

Live a legacy in order to leave a legacy.

Your giving should be a result of thought, preparation, and planning. Invest time into thinking about how you can make your giving sustainable by using it to create compounding value in the lives of others. Research the causes that incorporate sustainability into their practices. For example, give to the nonprofit that teaches communities to build water wells rather than simply providing them with clean water. And rather than just aiming to donate a certain amount every year, direct your charitable giving to efforts that will help people replicate the returns in their own and in others' lives.

In addition to making your gifts sustainable, a proactive giving plan ensures that you have the funds necessary to support your giving goals. Regardless of how much money you have, there will be never be anything left over to give away if you don't intentionally designate a portion of your income for charitable contributions. Creating a structured giving plan is the crucial step that will translate your goals and good intentions into gifts that lift others up.

Also, be mindful that you don't perceive giving as an unfortunate necessity. Possessions and finanical security are nice, but the most fun you will ever have with money is giving it away. Open yourself up to its rewards and you will experience all the riches of life in unprecedented ways.

All of us should give a piece of our time and a piece of our money, and if we're able to do that we'll cultivate an abundance mentality. You see, there are only two ways to think about time and money: abudance and scarcity. When Crystal admitted to feeling wealthy for the first time—I mean, truly understanding herself as being rich—after giving away $1 million, she was demonstrating the connection between generosity and an abundance mindset. Giving freely does not drain your resources; it makes you realize their plenitude, and it also attracts more abundance into your life.

What talent(s) do you have right now that you could share with others? How can you cultivate these talents to make these contributions larger over time? How should you budget your spending and saving to ensure you can hit your loftiest giving goals? In the Appendix, you'll find a section on "Your Giving Challenge," which will help you set your giving goals and actually meet them by implementing specific actions with your time, energy, and money every month.

Chapter Seven

STEWARDING RESOURCES NOW

It is literally true that you can succeed best and quickest by helping others succeed.
—NAPOLEON HILL

I had accomplished many of the goals that were on the list I made in that classroom with Crystal, but there was still one missing piece—the last item, where I had projected I would donate $1 million to a cause about which I was as passionate as that man digging wells in Africa. Keep in mind that when I wrote that goal, I had only $7 in my pocket. I had come a long way since then.

Then one day in the spring I was in a two-day board meeting at Oral Roberts University, and the president asked us to break into groups and challenged us to think about what we should be doing here at the university in the year 2030. Everybody threw out all kinds of different ideas, some of which related to extending campuses to Asia, Europe, Africa, South America, etc. Then one person chimed in and said, "You know, we should have a school of entrepreneurship. We already have an "Introduction to Entrepreneurship" class. We should build out our offerings in this area to include undergraduate and master's degrees and then export opportunities to people around the world."

We don't pursue inspiration or great ideas as much as they pursue us.

At the conclusion of the meeting, our ideas were all placed into a file and stored away, left to gather dust somewhere. But I just couldn't get away from the idea about the school of entrepreneurship. It wouldn't leave me alone. We don't pursue inspiration or great ideas as much as they pursue us. I couldn't shake this particular idea, and so I talked with Crystal about it and then I called Dr. Wilson, the president of the university, and told him I wanted him to come over to our house that afternoon.

I had conducted some research about what other schools of entrepreneurship around the country had done, and I told Dr. Wilson, "I have a vision for a project called the Stovall Center for Entrepreneurship. And if you and the board of trustees like it, I'll cut you a check for $1 million to launch it."

Well, Dr. Wilson took my ideas and went back to the trustees and the faculty, and they worked on it for a week or two. Then he came back to me, and he said, "We love your vision, and we've added some of our ideas to it and it's grown a little, so now it's going to cost $1.5 million."

So here I am, 59 years old, hearing those words Oral Roberts said 40 years ago in that chapel service about either giving your best and expecting the best or keeping your money, considering what sort of offering I will give. I turned to Crystal, and I said, "What do you think?"

She asked me, "Can we afford another half-million dollars?"

I told her, "We'll never miss it."

She said, "Well Jim, I think we ought to give him the money."

And we did. Almost exactly 40 years after I began my giving journey with that $10 donation to the missionary, I stood on stage in the ORU chapel and handed the president a check for $1 million, with an additional $500,000 to follow. After working together with other donors, we were able to raise another $500,000 and turn the Stovall Center for Entrepreneurship into a $2 million project. It's amazing how life comes full circle if we're on the path we're meant to be on.

After the check ceremony, Crystal and I had lunch with Dr. Wilson. He thanked us for our gift and informed us that there had been a development. He said, "There's a building across the street that the university used to own. They lost it, and it's passed through several owners. It was just acquired by an anonymous person, and they're donating it back to the university."

As he was describing it to me, I realized that it was the very same building in which my dad and Lee Braxton used to work and I used to hang out.

Dr. Wilson had been the president for only about five years, so he wouldn't have known the history of this building and its connection to our family. He asked us, "What would you think if the Stovall Center for Entrepreneurship was in that building?"

I looked at Crystal, and then I turned back to Dr. Wilson and said, "That's where the Center for Entrepreneurship started."

What an amazing feeeling to be able to walk my mom and dad, then 87 and 88 years old, through that building and show them the fruits of my education, their guidance, Mr. Braxton's mentorship, and the application of Hill's principles of achievement.

Years spent focusing on giving away $1 million kept my priorities straight—it kept me focused on what I could do for others, what value I could add to people's lives. Now all my goals relate to how Crystal and I are going to give away our money. They're not about getting another house or car. They're about supporting others' efforts to better themselves and their communities. One of the primary ways we do this is through the multiple scholarships we fund. There is nothing in the world like the feeling of sending a young person to college so that they can expand their mind, broaden their perspective, and learn the tools to transform their communities through whatever work they choose to do.

After Hurricane Dorian devastated the Bahamas, we fed 100,000 there. That's what really excites me. My ability to help others better their lives is what keeps me driven to reach my business goals. I know that in order to create the wherewithal to do that, you have to have the financial resources. But it's crucial not to wait until you've amassed a fortune before you begin the process. It doesn't work like that. If you're waiting until you've "made it" to make a contribution, you're going to be poor in spirit and in your pocketbook your whole life.

This philosophy of actively living a legacy so that others can discover and develop their gifts, create more fulfilling lives, and establish their own legacies is one shared by my good friend, Don Green. Under Don's leadership, the Napoleon Hill Foundation works every day to share the gift of Hill's success formula in ways that promote personal and community development through education.

With that in mind, the next section provides insight into the Foundation's efforts at continuing the legacy of Hill's success philosophy. It sheds light on how the Foundation's current activities—efforts with which I often partner—support the success journeys of budding entrepreneurs, individuals who face challenges like poverty or incarceration, and other innovative thinkers striving to institute positive change in their lives and society at large through hard work and dedication to a purpose greater than themselves.

As I write in *The Ultimate Gift*, "The only way you can truly get more out of life…is to give part of yourself away."[14] I hope that hearing Don's personal story intertwined with vignettes about the Foundation's giving strategies will illuminate the ways that very basic (and, as such, timeless) principles of personal achievement can have a massive impact—and one beyond the realm of individual financial gain.

Part II

THE LIVING LEGACY OF THE NAPOLEON HILL FOUNDATION

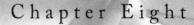

Chapter Eight

THE MESSAGE, NOT THE MAN

Life owes me nothing; I owe life
everything, and I am in the process of
paying off. I am paying it by throwing
out a life saver, so to speak, to those who
have been washed overboard, into the
waters of a restless, unsettled ocean of
life, where, on so many occasions in the
past, I found myself struggling for rescue.
—NAPOLEON HILL

It is wonderful to see the impact that Napoleon Hill's success principles have had on Jim Stovall and so many others around the world who have been inspired to better their lives and pay their gifts forward to their communities. Although so many focus on Hill and the products of his 20 years of research, during which time he interviewed over 500 of America's greatest minds and business people to formulate his Science of Personal Achievement, his true legacy is in his core message of self-empowerment through personal development, the tools he left behind for entrepreneurs and others to achieve success, and the lives of the individuals who have implemented his principles to cultivate and share their wealth and talent.

It is important to note that while Hill's extensive research and voluminous writings did eventually earn him monetary riches, there was absolutely no guarantee at the time that he agreed to the massive undertaking that he would benefit financially from it. The story of Hill's assignment goes like this: Andrew Carnegie, the great steel magnate, challenged Hill, then a poor regional journalist, to dedicate 20 years of his life to studying the successes and failures of America's wealthiest individuals and using that research to create a success formula that would help future generations. Carnegie noted that although the work would be unpaid, Hill would be sure to find riches along the way—conceivably, in the form of the insight gained and connections made. In his unpublished memoir, Hill chronicles the project's origins, writing, "I am conducting my research on my own time and at my own expense, without any form of financial backing, with the full knowledge that a major portion of the benefits of my labor will go to others, many of them not yet born."[15]

The last portion of that quote—"many of them not yet born"—merits additional consideration. Not only did Hill recognize from the outset that his life's work was intended to benefit others, but he realized that the timeless principles he would uncover would form a success philosophy that would inspire countless generations to come to live out their own legacies. He continues by suggesting that his research would reveal "new knowledge that will be of enduring benefit to the schools and colleges."[16] Although his Science of Personal Achievement is often left out of traditional curricula, he was essentially correct in his predictions, for the lasting value of the tools he discovered is evident in the number of prosperous entrepreneurs, thought leaders, and cultural icons who cite his message as a major factor in their success. To name just a few: Charlie "Tremendous" Jones, founder of Executive Books; Daymond John, founder and CEO of FUBU apparel and co-star of ABC TV's *Shark Tank*; Les Brown, motivational speaker and author; S. Truett Cathy, founder of Chick-fil-A; Tony Robbins, life and business strategist; comedian and businessman Steve Harvey; and Steve Forbes, editor-in-chief of *Forbes* magazine.

As the executive director and CEO of the Napoleon Hill Foundation, I know the enduring value of Hill's message, but I never tire of hearing about how it helps people succeed and use their success for a greater purpose. Read the story of any person who names one of Napoleon Hill's books as a reason for their success, and you will find that they grew their value while being driven to add value to others.

Take S. Truett Cathy, for instance. Cathy, who revolutionized the fast food industry with the founding of Chick-fil-A, said, "I was introduced to *Think and Grow Rich* as a high school student. It gave me a new lease on life when I realized I could do anything if I had the desire and believed I could achieve my goals."[17] His teacher gave him a copy in 1937, and for the rest of his life he carried around two books: *Think and Grow Rich* and the Bible.

Chick-fil-A brought Cathy great financial success, but profit was perhaps secondary to the main riches created by his business model: charity. At the time of his passing in 2014, his company had given over $68 million to charities and scholarships since its founding, and it continues its philanthropic efforts under his son Dan's leadership to this day.[18] Cathy did not store his wealth to wait until some undetermined future time to leave a legacy; he lived out his legacy every day in his gifts to over 700 educational and charitable organizations, his investment in developing his employees through scholarship funds, and his commitment to keeping the restaurant chain closed on Sundays so that employees could spend time with their families.

Indeed, at the heart of Chick-fil-A was a larger vision of service to his employees, the community, and the world. Cathy is quoted as saying: "I'd like to be remembered as one who kept my priorities in the right order. We live in a changing world, but we need to be reminded that the important things have not changed. I have always encouraged my restaurant operators and team members to give back to the local community. We should be about more than just selling chicken, we should be a part of our customers' lives and the communities in which we serve."[19]

As with Cathy, Charlie "Tremendous" Jones used the insight gained from Hill's writings to build a remarkable career dedicated to improving others' lives through reading. Beyond inspiring millions of people around the world through the books he wrote and edited, Jones was a remarkable philanthropist who earned the honor of the 2006 Nido Qubein Philanthropist of the Year Award from the National Speakers Association. His daughter Tracey continues to share his legacy in her messages, explaining one of her father's Seven Laws of Leadership, "Give to Get," in the following manner: "If I give something just to get something, that's not truly giving. That's trading." She continues: "Prosperity isn't only about your paycheck. Prosperity is about becoming a richer person because you're a giver....It's like being an organ donor while you're still living. How much of myself can I donate while I'm living to make people's lives better?"[20]

How much of myself can I donate while I'm living to make people's lives better?

Tracey's analogy beautifully captures the importance of legacy-building while you are still alive rather than waiting until all is said and done to give back. The impulse to raise people up into better conditions and to help people get the most out of their lives is at the core of Hill's work, and it is why so many of the beneficiaries of Hill's legacy, like Jim Stovall himself—who joins Jimmy Carter, Nancy Reagan, and Mother Teresa in having the incredible honor of being named International Humanitarian of the Year—have success journeys that integrate both traditional entrepreneurship with social entrepreneurship. Similar to Jim, Steve Forbes is known as having celebrated the enormous impact of Hill and for positioning philanthropy at the forefront of his work as an entrepreneur, sharing with *The Washington Post* his belief that "Today's challenges require individuals willing to invest capital and leadership without the expectation of personal gain, but instead with a focus on public welfare."[21]

Another powerful example of the legacy of Hill's message is the life of W. Clement Stone. Stone started in the insurance industry with only $100 in cash and a copy of *Think and Grow Rich*. He and Hill met in 1953, and Stone asked Hill to help train his employees in the Science of Personal Achievement. With help from Hill and his book, Stone built an insurance empire and amassed a $500 million fortune, which he intended to use to benefit humankind. He is known to have said, "All I want to do is change the world." And benefit humankind he did—over his lifetime, he gave more than $275 million to charities ranging from mental health organizations to youth welfare groups. But beyond his financial generosity, he lived his legacy in the way he used his leadership position to help others better their lives, hiring people like himself who had a limited education and raising their job prospects through training and sales opportunities.

Stone's generosity and commitment to helping others attain their goals also found expression in his long-term involvement with and financial support of the Napoleon Hill Foundation, a nonprofit educational organization dedicated to perpetuating Hill's success philosophies and making the world a better place in which to live.

When Stone sought to hire me to serve as the executive director and CEO of the Napoleon Hill Foundation, the organization was headquartered in Northbrook, Illinois. But I always felt that the Foundation would best fulfill its mission by being firmly embedded in the community in which Hill was born and raised—Wise, Virginia. This is a coal-mining region and one that is characterized by poverty and low levels of formal education, but it is one that also houses the University of Virginia's College at Wise. As the executor of Hill's intellectual legacy, I felt it was very important to build the university and the Wise community with the gifts that Hill and Stone left behind, so I recommended that we relocate the headquarters of the Foundation to Wise. Since then, the Foundation has committed to serving the Wise community while also producing products that better others' lives and generate financial profit, money that can be used to better the world through scholarships, outreach programs, lincensing opportunities, and more.

As Hill discovered, selfless dedication to improving the lives of others is the ultimate key to success. Writing in *Grow Rich! with Peace of Mind*, an excerpt of which is provided in the Appendix, Hill instructs, "Make sure your work and your money benefit someone besides yourself."[22] The Foundation exists to continue Hill's mission of supporting entrepreneurs in creating and living out their legacies. If Hill were here today, he would emphasize that he was a medium for something much bigger than himself: a message that will continue to inspire countless generations to better themselves through education and application and, in so doing, achieve greatness.

OPPORTUNITY: THE FRUIT OF OPTIMISM

One optimist may wield more constructive influence than a thousand pessimists.
—NAPOLEON HILL

I t is a great blessing to share the wealth we have accumulated over the years. It is an even greater blessing to realize that there is a great wealth in sharing a part of ourselves with those around us, no matter what stage of life we find ourselves in.

I firmly believe that all manner of blessings come to those who are guided by a spirit of optimism. It is the bedrock of both a solid success philosophy and an effectual giving plan. As Hill instructs, "Send out positive thoughts from a positively oriented soul and the world will reflect back greater and greater positive influences to help you."[23]

My mother set a strong example for me about how to live a legacy through a spirit of optimism. Although we were poor, living in rural Appalachia, which struggles with unemployment and generational poverty, every day my mother woke up with the most pleasant outlook, grateful for her life and ready to pay forward her gifts in any way that she could. She was known for constantly contacting people to see if she could help them—drive them to an appointment, help them run an errand, you name it. She got a new van just so she could transport people wherever they needed to go. My mother exemplified what it means to be generous with your time and energy and demonstrated the need to prioritize service by taking consistent action every day.

You know, some people always say, "Let me know what I can do to help." How many of us actually mean that? Few individuals are actually going to give you specific ways to help, even if they're in desperate need.

My mother paid attention to what people around her might need and offered concrete suggestions for ways that she could help.

Consider the people you know. What are some of the needs they likely have? If you're not sure, spend some time throughout the week observing your friends, co-workers, neighbors, etc., through the mental framework of service and generosity, and identify potential needs they might have based on what you notice. What are some specific ways to meet these needs that you could suggest to them? A specific offer of help is less likely to be turned down than a vague one that seems to emerge from politeness instead of genuine empathy.

Growing up with this example during my childhood and adolescence helped me extend my mom's legacy, as it trained me to practice situational awareness, like her. Now it is habitual for me to put myself out there in the world, identify people whom I could assist, and then create a plan to help them. I have a sign by my breakfast table that reads: "God, show me someone I can help today. In Jesus' name. Amen." I love this prayer because it serves as an extra reminder to attune myself to possible needs I might encounter throughout my day and to consider how I might respond to them by sharing my time, money, or talent.

As the executive director and CEO of the Napoleon Hill Foundation, I am privileged to be able to meet people from so many different walks of life and from all areas of the world. What unites us all is our desire to make our lives meaningful—to be purposeful with the time we've been given on this earth, to leave a legacy so that the world is better having had us in it—and our belief in the power of Hill's message to help us carry out our greater purpose. Hill himself wrote in his autobiography, "I have great faith in the future of America, and share, to no extent whatsoever, the feeling of defeatism which has spread itself over this country in recent years."[24] We at the Foundation share this belief in the greatness within humankind and the optimistic expectation that when people have the tools they need to develop their talents, they can transform their lives and the world in which they live. It is in this spirit that we join in Hill's mission to "live entirely in the present and in the future," with "the utmost faith that the service I shall render the world in the future will be incomparably greater than anything I have done in the past."[25] Every day I have the opportunity to use Hill's message to uplift others. It might be giving one of his books to someone I meet, or it might entail offering my time to speak with a group of students. With a heart and mind intent on serving, the chances to give are endless.

Recently, I met a man for dinner who was visiting from Colombia. He traveled by plane to Florida and then drove all the way to Wise, Virginia, to deliver a check for the licensed program he implemented in his native country. This gentleman wants to share Hill's tools for success with those in his community so that they can better their lives. We need more of these types of people who use their work to build others up. At dinner, he admitted to me that he did not own a tie. I own over a hundred ties and haven't worn many of them in years, so I gave him four from my collection. This was a small gift compared with the work the Foundation and philanthropists like Jim do, but even the smallest act of service can make a huge difference in someone's life.

With a heart and mind intent on serving, the chances to give are endless.

Even just encouraging people can produce dramatic results. Once I asked a professor at UVa Wise, "What's the biggest thing that holds kids back in college?" He responded, "A lack of self-confidence." Oftentimes, this hasn't been developed in kids because of their home life or experience in school. But until children build self-confidence, it will be difficult for them to achieve anything outstanding. That is why the Foundation places such a significant emphasis on education. By making educational opportunities accessible to students in our community and by sharing the Science of Personal Achievement globally, we hope that people will develop the confidence they need to boldly pursue their dreams and, *as* they do—not *after* they do—help others to do the same.

I identified early on that education and the power of books would be essential to my personal giving journey. While I was a bank president—a position I held for almost 20 years—I developed a course based on Napoleon Hill's success principles. I told the chairman of the board at the bank, who was also the chairman of the board at UVa Wise, about my interest in teaching this course and asked if he could introduce me to the people in the business school whose approval I would need. He told me he could arrange the meeting but that the other professors might be resistant to a non-academic coming in and teaching in their program. I planned out a syllabus in which each of the 17 success principles, starting with definiteness of purpose, would be taught. The chairman passed the syllabus and the textbooks on to the business school faculty, who read the materials and agreed to insert the course into the curriculum—*if* I would teach it myself.

I taught it 12 times until they were able to find someone else qualified to teach it. I was still working as a bank president during the day and then would teach this course one night a week. It attracted a range of students. In my first class, my students included a husband and wife who worked together at a bank, along with their two twin boys; a pediatrician; a pharmacist; a CPA; and a lawyer, among many others. The diversity of the class attests to the wide-ranging application of Hill's principles across all industries, disciplines, and lifestyles. The message behind the Science of Personal Achievement truly transcends boundaries created by time, geography, and background. I had 52 people sign up for my first class, which UVa Wise tried to prevent because they pride themselves on small class sizes. But I told them I wanted as many people as possible to hear these lessons. And it was a very popular course the whole time I taught it. I made so many friendships that have lasted a lifetime.

When I received my payment for the course, I would endorse the check and return it to the College. You see, it was never about the money; it always was about sharing the essential building blocks of success with those invested in bettering themselves. It was just icing on the cake that I was able to further this mission by returning the money back to the college. To this day, that course—"Keys to Success"—is still active. And just like Hill's philosophy, it is community oriented: a capstone project invites students with a GPA of 3.0 or higher to participate in a community program and talk to inmates, kids in the juvenile detention system, young men and women making use of Job Corps, etc., about one specific principle from the Science of Success.

It's amazing how giving with that spirit of optimism creates a snowball effect, where additional opportunities to prosper and to give back emerge as the offspring of our generosity. A young man in the first class I ever taught helped me start Napoleon Hill Day, an occasion that has taken on a life of its own. UVa Wise organizes a series of events that culminates with a keynote address by a contemporary thought leader whose journey has been shaped by Hill's message. This speech is free to the public and is meant especially for local high school and college kids, who are able to get to know a bit about Hill's philosophy and the university while receiving encouragement to take action on their dreams. The speech is also unpaid, so the keynote speakers donate their time and talent by participating.

One of the keynote speakers was Joe Dudley, an American businessman who has given away millions of dollars to support African-American entrepreneurs. He faced many obstacles growing up, including a speech impediment that caused him to be the recipient of discrimination and low expectations. His high school girlfriend said she couldn't marry him because she was worried that their kids would have mental disabilities. Of course, there's no connection between speech impediments and cognitive impairments, but that was how the world perceived him. He read *Think and Grow Rich* 300 times, and it completely transformed his life. As he built the incredibly successful company Dudley

Products Inc., he met with his employees every week to discuss Hill's principles. And rather than wait to leave a legacy at the end of his life, he donated his time in speaking at prisons, at shelters, and of course at Napoleon Hill Day, and he created a structured plan of giving through the foundation that he and his wife established.

Jim Stovall was also a keynote speaker at Napoleon Hill Day one year, and his story about not letting his disability hold him back from success was very inspirational for the students. In it, he talks about how in the early days of his vision loss, he would sit at the phone, tape recorder, and radio, questioning his ability to even get the mail, but with his focus firmly locked on his goals, he made it to the end of the driveway and continued to set progressively higher goals, until one day he's speaking to thousands of people at Madison Square Garden. It's truly a remarkable story. After Jim's speech, a little boy with a disability told his family, "If that blind man can do something with his life, I can too." Another girl decided that despite being raised in poverty, she could make something of her life.

Napoleon Hill Day has a remarkable influence on the students. The teachers all attest to how it instills confidence in the young people who attend, making them realize that regardless of their origins, they can make something great out of their life. And it also affirms the importance of seeking to add value to others' lives, rather than just prospering financially. When these students begin to truly believe that they have talents and that these talents can be used to better their lives and improve their communities, they become incredibly motivated to study and work hard to make their dreams a reality. They receive the greatest gift of all—hope—which enables them to face fears, anxieties, and uncertainties and persist in their determination to actualize their vision of success.

Hope and its corollary, optimism, are the true legacy of Napoleon Hill, Jim Stovall, and others who have contributed to this essential Science of Success philosophy, and it is these gifts that the Foundation works to share through its business projects and philanthropic efforts.

With defeatism and low self-esteem the primary obstacles in the lives of so many, how does encouragement play a role in your giving and success journeys? How are you actively sharing the gifts of hope and optimism with those around you?

Chapter Ten

SUSTAINABLE GIVING: THE LEGACIES THAT LAST

In every soul there has been deposited
the seed of a great future, but that
seed will never germinate, much less
grow to maturity, except through
the rendering of useful service.
—NAPOLEON HILL

The most impactful legacies are the ones that are built and enjoyed during a person's lifetime, and the greatest giving plans are those that establish a framework for continued giving. If people receive the tools they need to support sustainable progress in their lives, rather than just a one-time handout, they are better equipped to create long-term, scalable change.

Living a legacy means supporting others to create their own path to giving.

Jim and I have giving philosophies that align in this way. We recognize that when our business efforts are backed by a desire to help other people succeed, we reap the benefits of financial prosperity and personal fulfillment.

When I was president of a community bank, it was my job to follow up with people who were defaulting on their mortgages. A lot of people take a very hard-line approach to this sort of position, going in and threatening to repossess the customer's home and belongings, but I viewed it as my role to help them solve their problems—not to solve their problems for them, but to give them the tools they needed to make the necessary changes in their life to support their personal success. I would tell them, "You and I both got a problem. I've got to satisfy the people in the office, and you've got to avoid foreclosure." If they were three payments behind on their mortgage, I would ask them if they could give just one of the three today, while I was there. If they had lost their job or were unable to make any payments for another reason, I'd recommend that they sell their house, rather than losing it to the bank, who would take their down payment. If they listed it, they could at least recoup a little bit of money. Because of this, they would work with me, rather than hide from me, so that we could both solve each other's problems.

It's amazing what people will do when they know you're on their side. While I was in the banking business, I never foreclosed on one home loan. Prior to my working there, that community bank had 35 foreclosed homes on their books. I sold every single one of those 35 homes, most of them without a down payment, because I met people where they were at and established a structure for their success as homeowners. I invited people in—some of them the very ones who had lost these homes to begin with—and set them up on 15-year loans. The bank's trustees wondered, "How can you sell them houses with no money down?" I'd tell them, "We at least got them back on the books, accruing interest. Once you foreclose, the bank gets no income at all." It really is good business to operate within a framework of service and to establish systems in which people can pick themselves up and create a good life for themselves.

You can build a structure of support like this by donating your time or talent—for example, volunteering to read children books that will set them on the right path by helping them realize their greatness. If you're a hair stylist, you could volunteer at a homeless shelter by providing free haircuts, which will help the residents look more professional for job interviews. Because of the haircut, they're given the confidence and the polished appearance they need to obtain a job and earn an income that will help them get off the street. You don't need money to make a difference.

Jim is a great example of how you can share your talents to create sustainable change in people's lives. He has been such a gift to the Foundation and the college here: in addition to not charging us a speaking fee, he doesn't even bill for the hotel or travel. He donates the proceeds of his *Wisdom for Winners* books to the Foundation—and is doing the same with any profits from this one—so that we can extend the reach of Hill's philosophy through his and others' work. Jim recognizes how books can open up a whole new world for their readers, and so it's been wonderful to partner with him in sharing this opportunity with readers around the globe.

But money can make a huge difference as well, and just like Jim uses his wealth to bless others through structured giving programs, the Foundation aims to develop the Wise community and the larger world by equipping them with the tools they need to succeed.

One of the primary ways we do this is through our many scholarship programs. A large portion of the UVa Wise students require financial support to make college possible for them. Eighty percent receive some form of financial assistance. Sixty-eight percent qualify for federal aid. Fifty-five percent receive no contributions from their family to help them live above the poverty line. Over the past 30 years, however, the Foundation has awarded hundreds of scholarships to help students with financial need attend the college here. Originally, my uncle, who had a fourth-grade education, donated about $540,000 to the College to establish a scholarship fund. I have managed this money and grown it through investments and donations so that our current endowment is over $1 million. My wife and I also have set up a continued giving plan so that our own savings can support the growth and sustainability of the scholarship program. Last year alone the Foundation was able to award 22 scholarships. Now with the recent scholarship that Jim established in honor of his late mother, we'll be able to provide even more support for students here.

These scholarships have a massive, long-term impact. Because of them, UVa Wise has been recognized by *U.S. News & World Report* as having the second lowest debt load carried by students out of all the four-year colleges in the United States. When these students can focus on their studies without having to worry about where their next meal is going to come from, and when they can finish school without debilitating amounts of student loan debt, they are able to catapult themselves into higher levels of personal and professional achievement, which ultimately benefits their towns and the larger world.

The Foundation also partners with a number of community and international programs to help people get themselves out of cycles of generational poverty, unemployment, and imprisonment. Our office continuously boxes up Napoleon Hill Foundation books and sends them around the world. We contribute to eight free lending libraries around town, and we furnish the other local libraries with donated books. In addition, we partner with Sound Wisdom to give away books to prison reading programs. Together we've donated thousands of books—totaling hundreds of thousands of dollars in retail value—to share the Science of Personal Achievement. We've received letters from inmates expressing their gratitude for the program and detailing how Hill's message enabled them to see themselves for the first time as worthy and capable of making something of themselves. If we can help even one person break out of a cycle of poverty and criminality, we know we've created a ripple of positive change with wide-reaching effects. To date, we've given away over $1 million in books and curriculum products to individuals in impoverished areas around the world.

One of the most meaningful examples of the impact of our prison reading program occurred when we published *Outwitting the Devil* in 2011. A man with a radio program in Detroit, Michigan, called me to request an interview. He said he would even pay for a press release, which he did—and it ended up in about 200 newspapers just as the book was released. All the local stores sold out of the book when it hit the shelves. After we had our on-air conversation, the gentleman asked me to stay on the line. He said, "Don, you're probably wondering why I did all this for you."

I told him, "You're right. You've gone out of your way to publicize the release of our book. Why?"

He responded, "You've been sending my son books."

I asked him, "What's his name?"

He told me, and I recognized it. But he had a different last name than the broadcaster. The radio personality told me that he changed his name after his son committed murder as a young man. It was a tragic story. The young man paid heavily for what he did in a moment of bitterness and ended up with a life sentence. He served 20-odd years in prison, and during that time he decided that he would completely turn his life around if and when he got out. He set a goal of reading 500 books a year, and he was particularly taken with the Napoleon Hill titles. He wrote us letters for years. I eventually wrote him a support letter when he went up for parole. By the time he left prison, he had earned both bachelor's and master's degrees. Since then, he's been working in construction.

There are all kinds of stories like this one, even going back to the days of Bill Sands, a man who by his nineteenth birthday was serving three consecutive life terms in San Quentin for drug charges before he was eventually pardoned by the governor of Arkansas. He discovered Hill's success formula and completely turned his life around, going from being on the verge of committing murder to becoming a successful businessman, famous speaker, and author of a best-selling book. He delivered over 3,000 speeches to high schools telling students to read books and stay away from bad influences. One of the last acts President Reagan did in office was pardon Sands and reinstate his voting rights because of the massive impact he had on the lives of so many at-risk youth.

This is the power of Hill's message, which we want to magnify by giving it the greatest reach possible. At the Foundation, we believe there are only two ways to learn: books and the association with people who are smarter than we are. If we don't read much, then we're off to a bad start. If our social environment is bad, then we're off to a really bad start. But all of that can be changed. All of us—not just the Foundation—can work at it by sharing our time with people, refusing to give up on them, and providing them with viable opportunities and strategies for digging themselves out of the limiting circumstances they've been given. You never, ever want to discard a human being as not worthy of assistance—you never know what they can contribute. Look at Napoleon Hill: he had been told for years that he was a young rascal who would never do anything with his life, but when his stepmother came into his life and told him she saw a great future for him, he completely turned his life around and left the world with a revolutionary success philosophy.

There are so many opportunities to share our resources in ways that will help people better their lives. One lady recently wanted to take one of our courses, but she couldn't afford it so I mailed her a few books. We received the most touching response from her. There's a chance to do something like that every day—in countries beyond America as well. Once we were contacted by people in Iran about licensing our books, and we offered them a discounted price so that they could share Hill's message with their country. We have at least 25 books licensed in Saudi Arabia, and we do not make as much of a margin on those books as we would from a European country. We want to make a difference in those countries, but we benefit as well from the associations. We build friendships.

People wonder how we can afford to give away so many books and discounted licenses, but it is always the case, as the Book of Proverbs says, that those who give freely will be made richer and those who withhold will suffer in some way, even if only emotionally. The Golden Rule is the truest philosophy ever to grace the earth: whatever you give comes right back to you—not necessarily in the sense that if you give $10,000 you'll get $20,000 back, but you receive the reward of feeling like you've done a great deed, you've released the bondage of hatred or jealousy or greed, and you develop peace of mind, the greatest form of wealth that exists, as Napoleon Hill discovered later in life. With peace of mind, you have enhanced creativity because thoughts of money, greed, and consumption are not weighing you down. Some people make a god out of their money, and nothing they ever earn or buy is enough. Hill was very clear that peace of mind comes from mastering money rather than letting it master you.[26] And the way to master money is to make sure it's being put to work to help others. Remember, you can't take it with you. I've never seen a U-Haul carrying funeral possessions to heaven.

However, if you use your resources to establish or maintain structures that support people's long-term growth, you can enjoy your gifts now. Rather than leaving a legacy, you can live one every single day in the deeds you do, the words you share, and the gifts you give. You don't have to fund a scholarship or sponsor a community program or anything like that to make a difference, so don't wait until you've amassed a fortune to enjoy the gift of giving. Use the guide in the Appendix to create your giving plan, identifying actions you can take now, in the near future, and in the long run to create systemic change and reach your ultimate giving goal. However, when identifying this ultimate giving goal, don't limit yourself either: you'll be amazed at what incremental steps, savings, acts of service, and donations can add up to over the years.

Whether it's sharing your time, your talent, or your treasure, decide today how you will change your life and the world through the gift of giving. Your ultimate giving journey begins now...

Appendix

CREATING YOUR GIVING PLAN

THE LIVING LEGACY OF C. BASCOM SLEMP

C. Bascom Slemp is a powerful example of living a legacy. I felt this story was important to share because Slemp not only modeled what sustainable giving looks like, but he also committed resources to bettering the lives of Southwest Virginians, like the Napoleon Hill Foundation currently does. I had the opportunity to tour Slemp's personal library and was moved to discover an original copy of *Think and Grow Rich* within his collection. While we do not know how integral Hill's book was to Slemp's giving journey, it is clear that his legacy aligns with Hill's message of using the power of reading and education to improve people's circumstances.

—DON GREEN

Some give freely, yet grow rich; others withhold what is due and only suffer.

—PROVERBS 11:24

Campbell Bascom Slemp was born on September 4, 1870, and died on August 7, 1943. He was an American politician and a six-time United States congressman from Virginia's ninth district from 1907 to 1923. He also served as presidential secretary to President Calvin Coolidge.

Slemp attended the "seminary" in rural Turkey Cove, Virginia, that was operated by the Methodist Church there. He also had a private tutor who was a college professor. At age nine, he became a page in the Virginia House of Delegates after his father was elected to the Virginia General Assembly. At age 16, C. Bascom Slemp entered the Corp of Cadets and Virginia Military Institute in Lexington, Virginia. He graduated from there in 1891 with the highest grade point average in the school's history—a record that still stands today. Later on, Slemp studied law at the University of Virginia and after one year was admitted to the bar. After his terms as congressman and presidential secretary, Slemp decided to move to Big Stone Gap, Virginia, and resumed his law practice. He also had numerous ventures in real estate and coal and lumber operations. With the help of his sister, his mansion in Big Stone Gap was established as the Southwest Virginia Museum and became part of the Virginia State Park system. This building is a large stone mansion built by General Rufus Ayers, Napoleon Hill's first employer.

Even after his passing, Slemp continues to touch the lives of Southwest Virginians through his philanthropy. He established the Slemp Foundation in his will that provides gifts to libraries, schools, and colleges in Southwest Virginia. The Slemp Scholarship is awarded to outstanding college students who graduated from Lee, Scott, and Wise County Virginia high schools.

In October 2003, the University of Virginia's College at Wise created a five-story student center with a $2.5 million gift from the Slemp Foundation. This building was named the Slemp Student Center in C. Bascom Slemp's honor. Additionally, it is astounding that the University of Virginia's College at Wise students graduate with the second lowest level of student debt in the nation. This is due in part to the generous contributions from benefactors such as the Slemp Foundation.

JIM STOVALL'S WISDOM FOR GIVERS ON LIVING A LEGACY

"Whether it's in our personal or professional lives, we need to think about giving as an integral part of all that we do instead of an afterthought. Giving back is a way to create a true and lasting legacy. A lot of people do a good job of making money, and most everyone does a good job of spending it. But it's the giving of one's money that will yield a far more valuable return on investment."

From "Giving"

"If you and I can find a way to go beyond simply doing something in this life, or even leaving something behind, we can expand our impact into planting seeds that will bear fruit long after we are gone."

From "The Legend Lives On"

"Everyone builds our legacy one day at a time. Often we think of a legacy as something elderly people contemplate at the end of their lives, but our legacy is our life's work that is projected into the impact it has on other people and generations to come."

ooooo

"Success comes when we realize life is not just about us but involves others around us. Legacy takes it one step further and introduces the consideration of impacting people we may never know and generations not yet born. If we focus on our own gratification, we make poor decisions; if we think of others, we make good decisions; but if we contemplate our permanent legacy, we can approach greatness."

From "The Ultimate Legacy"

"I have long believed that the meaning of life is to find our gift, and then we achieve purpose and significance when we give it away."

From "Practice and Perfection"

"If you forego a luxury item you want and give to someone else so that they can buy a luxury item for themselves that doesn't impact anyone else, you will not make yourself or the person receiving your gift as happy as could have otherwise been possible; however, if you give gifts to people who utilize that gift to serve others in a way that can impact society into the future, you can multiply and share the happiness money generates. Whether it's time, love, resources, or money, the way to enjoy it best is to share it with others."

From "Money Can Make You Happy"

On Giving of Ourselves

"Giving does not simply apply to our money but includes our time, effort, energy, and our expertise. Any of us can give our money, and it is greatly needed and appreciated by people and causes around the world. But only you can provide a unique effort, energy, and expertise that you can bring to a particular need."

From "Giving"

"Truly successful people all understand that giving is a gift. We all have opportunities to give of our time or our money, but on a few special occasions, we have a chance to give of ourselves…. Whether you're at the stage of your life where you're giving time or money, always look for occasions when you can give a part of yourself. Something as simple as a home cooked meal, a handwritten note, or something born out of your own creative talents will provide the most benefit and longest lasting impact."

From "Giving of Yourself"

"We're all planting seeds every day. Not only in our own lives, but in the lives of people around us. These seeds don't add. They multiply. So if you do something for someone else and they pass it on, by the end of the day, the random act of kindness that you have paid forward could touch the lives of thousands of people. When we do things for others not expecting to benefit, we inevitably receive a mental and spiritual benefit, but often we also receive an unexpected benefit."

From "Paying It Forward"

"If we want to make people really happy, we need to look beyond just the standard stuff we buy at the mall, wrap up, and hand to someone. We need to explore the concept of sharing an experience, giving of ourselves, or engaging in a giving activity with our loved ones."

From "Holiday Happiness"

"In our personal and professional lives, we have the opportunity to reach out to hundreds of people every day—with an encouraging word, an act of kindness, or by simply taking a few moments to truly listen and help. We, as professionals, have a responsibility to positively impact the lives of others not only with our products and services, but by our examples. How much more effective we can be if, from time to time in the midst of our search for excellence, we stop to light a torch and pass it on to another messenger."

From "Passing the Torch"

On Goal-Setting and Decision-Making

"Life is more like an ongoing highway than a series of short steps, but sometimes we need to pull into a rest stop and examine where we are, where we've been, and, more importantly, where we're going. Always remember that these milestones are not just for you. As the great poet John Donne told us so eloquently, no one is an island."

From "Cutting the Ribbon"

"If you have a goal, a dream, or a destiny in your life that you would like to reach, you should be making progress toward it today. That progress may involve taking significant strides toward those things you want to be, do, or have, or it may simply mean reading a book, meeting a person, improving your attitude, or any number of things that can put you in the right position to move forward immediately when the opportunity presents itself."

From "Always Move Forward"

"Often...it is hard to get away from the day-to-day rush and really think about the things that are important. We are so busy making a living we forget to create a life. The life we're living right now is not a practice game. This is the Super Bowl and the World Series and the Olympics all rolled up into one. If you do not feel that kind of power and passion each day of your life, this would be a good time to dust off those old dreams and find your unique and fulfilling place in this world."

From "The Gift of Dreams"

"Too many of us are guilty of assuming that we don't have all of the pieces necessary to reach our goals. Complaints of 'If I only had the education or time or contacts or money, etc.' are often heard. Please understand that sometimes there are legitimate barriers between us and our success, but too often there are convenient challenges that masquerade as handy excuses for our remaining in the rut we find ourselves…. Today, resolve to move toward your destiny assuming that everything you need you already have or you expect it to be provided for you at the point you need it most."

From "Assume You Have What You Need"

"Success in business, finances, or life in general comes from making good decisions. Good decisions are products of saying yes to the right things that require us to say no to everything else."

From "Just Say No"

"Delaying a decision diminishes our choices. Avoiding a decision entirely transfers our right to choose to someone else; but never forget, we always live with our decisions whether we make them promptly or avoid them entirely."

From "Avoiding Decisions"

On Managing Our Resources

"Acquiring wealth requires purpose and focus. Unless there's something you want to specifically do with money, there is no reason to have it. The only three items you can spend your money on are things, memories, and security. A portion of every dollar you have should be spent on your current needs, a portion should be saved and invested for your future needs, and a portion of every dollar should be given away.

"Most people spend all they earn and a little bit more via consumer debt having little or no savings or investments for the future and rarely, if ever, think about giving. Constant and habitual giving is another indicator of an abundance mentality. Only those who believe they either have or are in the process of acquiring abundance, can freely give to others. Before you change your spending budget, your investment plan, or your retirement vehicle, change your attitude regarding money. You can never out-earn, out-save, or out-invest a scarcity attitude. If you believe you are destined to always struggle financially, you will create the circumstances to meet your expectations. On the other hand, if you envision yourself living a life of abundance and providing for people and causes that you care about, your thoughts will manifest themselves in your life."

From "Being Happy for the Joneses"

"In order to begin to have healthy attitudes toward money, we must understand that it is nothing more or less than a tool or a vehicle. Money can get us what we want or take us where we want to go. Unless there is something you want or somewhere you wish to go, money has no value."

From "The Gift of Money"

"How we spend our time and how we spend our money reveal our thoughts and the underlying priorities…take control of your thoughts to an extent where they take control of your actions and provide the results you desire."

From "Thoughts, Actions, and Results"

"The pursuit of money is a road that leads to dissatisfaction and, quite often, financial ruin. The pursuit of passion invariably leads to happiness, satisfaction, and financial success."

From "What You Do with What You Have"

"The idea of getting rich quick is a pipe-dream that robs your resources and your possibilities. Creating a wealth plan provides a certainty over time of financial freedom and success."

From "The Lack of Lottery Logic"

"There are only three things we can do with our money: invest it, spend it, or give it away. A portion of every dollar should be directed toward each of these areas. Money that we spend today can meet our current needs and the needs of those around us. Money that we invest can meet these same needs in the future. But money we give away can make us happy now, for the rest of our lives, and leave a legacy behind long after we are gone."

From "Money Can Make You Happy"

"We often overlook issues of health, family, spirituality, and well-being when we establish our priorities. All things being equal,

THE GIFT OF GIVING

more money is better than less money, but if you're sacrificing your health or quality time with your loved ones for money, it is likely a poor bargain; we must, therefore, budget the things that are finite such as our time and money while prioritizing the elements of life that are infinite such as spirituality, well-being, and significance."

From "Two out of Three"

"If money is used properly, it can create great value in your life and in the lives of others; however if money is misused, it will take you farther away from the values that will truly make you happy."

From "Price vs. Value"

"The greatest myth about wealthy people is that they either inherited the money or won the lottery. In reality, over 90% of millionaires are first-generation millionaires who earned, saved, and invested their own money. People who win the lottery are more likely to file bankruptcy in the following 10 years than the average working-class person in our society. Therefore, with respect to wealth building, we must rely on the old adage: 'If it is to be, it is up to me.'"

From "Wealth 101"

On Success

"We live in a material world in which people seek instant gratification. They want to measure themselves based on what they have instead of who they are or what they do. What we have is a poor indicator of ourselves. The best indicator of success is simply who we are. This indicator is made up of the elements of our character, our personality, and our principles. The measure of who we are will lead to the second indicator, which is what we do. In this arena, we are judged by our efficiency, our productivity, and the contribution we make to the world. Only after we determine who we are and what we do can we impact what we have."

ooooo

"Success comes from being, then doing, which results in having. If you simply want to have more things without transforming who you are as a person and what you do as a service to the world, you are doomed to failure."

From "Transformation"

"Success comes when we plant seeds and don't worry about how or when we will get paid."

From "Paying It Forward"

"No one else can define your success any more than they can order your dinner, try on a suit of clothes for you, or tell your doctor where it hurts. When it comes to your personal and professional success, you determine the destination, the deadline, and the details. No one else can do this for you, and you must identify and define your own success if you ever hope to achieve it."

From "Identifying Success"

"Acquiring wealth and assets is a by-product of doing work that creates value in the lives of others."

From "Being, Doing, and Having"

"Never make having things or achieving status your goal. Instead seek to be the kind of person who will naturally do the right thing that will result in all of the things that our culture calls success."

From "You Are Not Your Performance"

"The world will give you fame, fortune, and acclaim if you simply recognize and solve other people's problems."

From "Stumbling to Success"

On Fulfillment

"When we think back on our lives about when we were truly happy, we discover it was at the times when we were expending our effort and energy in serving others and making them happy. Happiness is an elusive concept. To the extent we try to create it for ourselves, it avoids us, but to the extent we try to create happiness for others, it engulfs us. If we are committed to spending our time and effort in serving others and making them happy, and if we then add money to that equation, we can make many more people, and in turn ourselves, very happy."

From "Money Can Make You Happy"

"At its core, giving affects the receiver by virtue of the gift itself; but giving affects the giver in a much deeper and more lasting way. In the aftermath of an act of giving, the receiver has a new gift and the knowledge that someone cares deeply; but the giver has a new identity. He or she now has feelings of abundance, benevolence, and a sense of being able to make a difference."

From "The Gift of Giving"

"I am on an ongoing quest to catch people doing something right and let them know about it. This makes me feel better. It makes them feel better."

From "Balancing the Scales"

"The way to build a great life is simply to string together a series of great days. A great day can be defined as one in which, as you put your head on the pillow, you can reflect back over your day's activities and be satisfied. Ideally, you are not only satisfied with how well you did in pursuing your goal, but you are deeply satisfied that you are pursuing the right goal."

From "The Opinion That Counts"

On Mindset

"Everything you will ever do, know, have, give, and create first begins with a thought in your mind. Every good or bad thought can create an action and a corresponding result. If you want to change any aspect of your life, you first must change your mind."

From "A Change of Mind"

"If you maintain a good attitude and share it with everyone around you, you will be proven right most of the time, and you will enjoy a far better life."

From "Perspectives from the Past"

"If...we were willing to suspend our disbelief and dismiss skepticism, I believe that we would find a whole new world of possibility."

From "Suspending Disbelief"

THE BLESSED ART OF SHARING YOUR RICHES

BY NAPOLEON HILL

Wealth that is shared creates more wealth, and you can share many forms of wealth besides money. Today's millionaires themselves point out that anyone can become a millionaire because today's wealth is so widespread and gives rise to so many opportunities. When you share in your own home you create a basic harmony which adds to your success and peace of mind in everything you do. Start now to share what you have, and when you have plenty of money you will share your money more wisely and with greater benefit.

YOU are going to make money. If you do not allow negative points of view to trip you up, you will march straight forward on the road to riches. Yes, you are going to make money in solid sums—money that comes to you through your own worthy efforts—money you spend in helping others.

Will you build your character while you build your fortune? This, as by now you know, is not exactly "another matter." There is a strong connection between the power to make money and the power to know your own mind and fulfill your own self as a fully realized person.

Life proceeds according to the great Law of Compensation. The more you give of what you have, the more comes back to you—and it comes back greatly multiplied.

Again we shall examine a technique that goes with being rich and having invincible peace of mind. So far as sharing money is concerned, you may see this technique as belonging to your future. So far as sharing other forms of wealth is concerned, this technique is yours right now. Use it and make it part of you. Life proceeds according to the great Law of Compensation. The more you give of what you have, the more comes back to you—and it comes back greatly multiplied.

ooooo

Giving to those who help themselves.

Any man noted for his millions receives endless requests for money. He knows that most of these appeals come from people who will not use the money for necessities, let alone in any manner which helps them in their careers. He cannot hope to screen all such requests. Often it is far simpler for him to give large sums to a charity or to endow a foundation.

Those who have worked for their money know that the virtue of money consists in its use, not in its quantity. This is equally true whether the amount be a dime or a million dollars.

Henry Ford once was approached by Miss Martha Berry of the Martha Berry School in Georgia. Miss Berry asked for an endowment for her school, but Mr. Ford refused the request.

"Well," she countered, "will you give us a sack of peanuts?"

Mr. Ford obliged by buying her a sack of raw peanuts.

With the aid of her students, mountain boys and girls, Miss Berry planted and replanted the peanuts, selling the crop until she had converted the original sack into six hundred dollars in cash. She then returned to Mr. Ford and handed him the six hundred dollars, saying, "You see how practical we are in the use of money." Mr. Ford handed back the six hundred dollars, along with some two million dollars to build the fine stone buildings which now adorn the campus of the Martha Berry School in Mt. Berry, Georgia.

Mr. Ford made very few gifts of this kind. Experience had taught him that all too often gifts to schools are handled by impractical people who know very little about sound business (or farming) methods. As long as Martha Berry lived, the Ford private car appeared on the railroad siding near her school once a year, while Mr. and Mrs. Ford paid a visit.

A present-day multimillionaire, Henry Crown, who arrived in this country as a poor immigrant from Lithuania, is now a leading figure in the vast General Dynamics Corporation. Mr. Crown has put a great deal of money into a plan which teaches aspiring young people how to handle capital. He has set up a fund of eight thousand dollars at a good many colleges, and this money is invested each year by the senior economics class. When the class makes a profit, its members share the surplus, and the fund is passed on intact to the next class.

ooooo

Everyone has something to share and gains by sharing it.

When a stranger stops you in the street and asks directions, you share your knowledge when you tell him. You do not have to be rich in money in order to do this. If you are really rich in human kindness, you will give the stranger a very careful explanation, and perhaps walk to the next corner with him and point out the way.

The poorest of us has much to share. In some ways a poor man has as much to share as does a rich man. Certainly it is so with love and with kindness.

I shall suggest three general ways of sharing which are available to almost anybody. You may not make use of the particular instances used as examples, but the list will serve to open your mind to the many possibilities of sharing more than money.

1. Share your special skills or knowledge. Many of us possess some special skill or knowledge which helps us earn money. We are used to selling our skills. Now look for a way to give that skill without thought of gain.

A much-needed clubhouse for the boys was built in the slum section of a large city. The basic construction costs were provided by a large foundation, but the clubhouse never would have gotten started were it not for those who gave their skills. A lawyer volunteered his services in drawing up the incorporation papers and other necessary documents. A carpenter installed locker room partitions. A painter gave his own services and also supervised a volunteer crew which painted the entire interior in cheerful colors. A mason installed a concrete ramp at one entrance so that physically handicapped boys could make their way in.

2.   Share by filling a gap where you see one. Mr. A loaned his lawnmower to his new neighbor, Mr. B, who had not had time to equip himself. This was the beginning of excellent good-neighbor relations between the two families—but for a while, it seemed as though the matter were going the other way.

After Mr. B had trimmed his lawn, he returned the lawnmower with a big chip in one blade. Noticing this, Mr. A remarked diplomatically that Mr. B must have had some rocks hidden in his grass which chipped the blade. The new neighbor said gruffly that the blade had been chipped when he had been offered the use of the lawnmower, and walked away.

Since the chip was fresh and shiny, this hardly could have been so. Mr. A said nothing more, however. He limited his contacts with his new neighbor to mere nods if he met him in the street.

One day, Mr. B came around with a brand-new lawnmower and handed it to Mr. A. "I want you to have this," Mr. B said. "You see, I knew I'd broken that blade but I couldn't afford to have it fixed right then. I guess I should've said so, but, well, I didn't. Now things have turned out all right and I want to do more than merely have the blade fixed."

Thus is many a non-money debt returned with interest! Far more valuable than the lawnmower itself, however, was the atmosphere of cordiality which the two families found from then on.

3.   Share recognition and appreciation. Notice how often you are recognized as being in a certain role—for example, the role of a customer—and so you are treated in a certain way. Now turn around the situation and recognize the other person. You will find it is a limitless form of sharing.

For example, you may stop your car at a filling station on a hot day. The attendant rushes up, mopping his brow, anxious to give you prompt service. You recognize him as a person who has his own problems and you say: "Take it easy. It's too hot to hurry." He will remember you the next time you drive in.

Say you are an employer or a foreman. One of your men does exceptionally good work. Many an employer or foreman would observe that the man is paid to do a good job, so what? A wiser supervisor will make a point of telling a worker that his performance has been noticed. When a person does a good job, he is favorably disposed toward anyone who gives him recognition. Furthermore, he will try thereafter to keep his work up to a high standard.

You will offer a kindness, you will perform many a free service, and in many cases, you will see no return. Bear in mind there is always a return within yourself, for when you give of yourself you make yourself bigger. And remember the Law of Compensation which always works in your favor when you arrange it so. We shall look more deeply into the wonders of compensation later on.

In sharing, you will find you are wealthier than you think.

Look for ways to share your wealth. Never ask, "What wealth?" In sharing, you will find you are wealthier than you think. Share more than your money, and when you have plenty of money you will be more closely attuned to human needs and your money will give added benefit to those who share it.

The Supreme Secret is like a half-hidden treasure you may pass a hundred times a day without noticing; you see it from the corner of your eye.[27]

YOUR GIVING CHALLENGE

I t's time to identify your ultimate giving goal and commit to achieving it so that you can enjoy the fruits of your legacy while you are living. Dedicate time to thoughtful and sustained reflection on the questions below, which will enable you to locate the cause that lights your soul on fire and craft a giving plan that will ensure you are taking the steps you need to make your giving and success dreams a reality. As this Giving Challenge will help you realize, you do not need to wait until you've "made it" to begin sharing your gifts— your time, talent, and treasure—with the world. In fact, delaying your generosity is the surest way to lessen your impact and defer your own prosperity. As George Herbert famously said, "Do not wait: the time will never be 'just right.' Start where you stand, and work whatever tools you may have at your command and better tools will be found as you go along."[28]

Part I. Identifying Your Ultimate Giving Goal

1.   What are your passions? What truly matters to you?

_____

_____

_____

_____

_____

_____

_____

_____

_____

_____

_____

_____

2. What are your gifts/talents?

_____

_____

_____

_____

_____

_____

_____

_____
_____
_____
_____
_____
_____
_____
_____
_____

3. In what ways do your passions and gifts align in productive ways?

_____
_____
_____
_____
_____
_____
_____
_____
_____
_____
_____
_____
_____
_____
_____
_____

4.   How can these be used together to help people better their lives?

_____
_____
_____
_____
_____
_____
_____
_____
_____
_____
_____
_____
_____

5.   Do you have a passion that does not align with your gifts/talents about which you could develop knowledge through research or volunteering?

_____
_____
_____
_____
_____
_____

_____

_____

_____

_____

_____

_____

_____

_____

_____

_____

_____

_____

6. Based on your answers to questions 1–5, identify your giving focus and write it in the "Purpose Points" section below.

7. What nonprofits or other charitable organizations are already leveraging resources to better people's lives in this way?

    If you don't know, do some light research online.

_____

_____

_____

_____

_____

_____

_____

_____

_____

_____

_____

_____

_____

_____

_____

_____

8. How does your desire to give to this cause align
    with what these organizations are already doing?
    How does it differ?

_____

_____

_____

_____

_____

_____

_____

_____

_____

_____

9. Based on your passions, gifts/talents, and knowledge of what's already being done to benefit the cause most important to you, create your personal mission statement as it relates to giving in the "Purpose Points" below.

10. What are some ways that you could translate your mission into a sustainable gift?

   "Sustainable" means that the gift can continue to benefit others beyond the initial monetary donation or act of service. How can you make your money do work after it's been spent? How can your gift create exponential returns by equipping people to create positive change in their lives?

_____

_____

_____

_____

_____

_____

_____

11. What is the most rewarding manifestation of this sustainable gift that you can imagine? Your answer to this question becomes your ultimate giving goal, which you should write in the last line of the "Purpose Points" below.

    Remember, your highest giving goal does not need to be monetary in nature, though you should be giving a portion of every dollar you make to a charitable cause.

Purpose Points

Focus of giving:

_____

_____

_____

_____

_____

_____

This is the "cause" to which you'll contribute your resources. For example, Jim Stovall's focus has been education and entrepreneurship.

Mission statement:

Explain in one sentence how your purpose relates to the cause about which you are passionate. For example, Jim's mission is to support people in empowering themselves through entrepreneurial values to empower other people.

Ultimate giving goal:

_____

_____

_____

_____

_____

_____

_____

_____

_____

_____

_____

_____

_____

_____

_____

_____

_____

_____

This is the most rewarding contribution you can imagine making toward the focus you've selected. For Jim, it was donating $1 million to equipping entrepreneurs to solve tomorrow's problems today. However, it does not have to be strictly monetary in nature.

Anticipated date of ultimate gift:

_____ / _____ / _____

Part II. Sharing Your Resources

Time and Energy

1. How can you share your time and energy to reach your ultimate giving goal?

    What are volunteer opportunities that exist or that you can create to live out your giving mission now?

    _____

    _____

    _____

    _____

    _____

    _____

    _____

    _____

    _____

    _____

    _____

Talent/Gifts

1. How can you share your talent to reach your ultimate giving goal?

    How can you live out this giving mission now and in the future by sharing your knowledge, expertise, talents, and/or skills?

Financial/Tangible Resources

As Jim Stovall writes in Chapter 6, "Regardless of how much money you have, there will be never be anything left over to give away if you don't intentionally designate a portion of your income for charitable contributions. Creating a structured giving plan is the crucial step that will translate your goals and good intentions into gifts that lift others up." Keep the importance of a structured giving plan in mind as you go through the questions below and make a realistic plan for stewarding your financial resources so that you benefit your chosen cause.

1. Track your spending and saving activity for a month. Where are your financial resources going? Do these expenditures align with what truly matters to you?

    _____

    _____

    _____

    _____

    _____

    _____

    _____

    _____

    _____

    _____

    _____

    _____

2. How can you share your treasure (finances/tangible resources) to reach your ultimate giving goal?

    _____

    _____

    _____

    _____

    _____

    _____

_____

_____

_____

_____

_____

_____

_____

3. What line items in your budget can you eliminate
    or reduce to create extra room for saving, investing,
    and charitable giving?

    _Consider your answer to question 1 above when re-
    sponding to this question._

_____

_____

_____

_____

_____

_____

_____

_____

_____

_____

_____

_____

_____

4. How much of every paycheck will you set aside to save and invest right now?

   Remember to consider how giving plays a role in your savings goals, as your monthly savings and investments will help you reach your giving goals.

   _____

   _____

   _____

   _____

   _____

   _____

   _____

   _____

   _____

   _____

   _____

   _____

   _____

   _____

5. How much of every paycheck will you set aside for charitable giving right now?

   _____

   _____

Part III. Structuring Your Giving Journey

1. What is your deadline for this goal? Write your answer in the "Purpose Points" above.

    Make it realistic but within a short enough span of time that you can enjoy it.

2. What steps do you need to take today to reach this goal?

3. What steps do you need to take this month to reach this goal?

4. What steps do you need to take this year to reach this goal?

_____
_____
_____
_____
_____
_____
_____
_____
_____
_____
_____
_____
_____
_____
_____
_____
_____
_____

5. What steps do you need to take in the next ten
    years (or beyond) to reach this goal?

_____
_____
_____
_____
_____
_____

Part IV. Maintaining Motivation

1. In what ways does your ultimate giving goal align
    with your core values?

    _____

    _____

    _____

    _____

    _____

    _____

    _____

    _____

    _____

    _____

    _____

    _____

2. How will giving toward this cause bring enjoy-
    ment, satisfaction, peace, and other positive emo-
    tions into your life?

    _____

    _____

    _____

    _____

    _____

3. What will be the tangible and intangible benefits of your ultimate gift?

For yourself?

_____
_____
_____
_____
_____
_____
_____
_____
_____
_____
_____
_____

For your family and immediate network?

_____
_____
_____
_____
_____
_____
_____
_____
_____
_____
_____

_____

_____

_____

For your local community?

_____

_____

_____

_____

_____

_____

_____

_____

_____

_____

For the larger world?

_____

_____

_____

_____

_____

_____

4. Rather than "how do you want to be remembered," how do you want to be known right now?

5. Who can support you in reaching your ultimate giving goal?

Who can support you by offering encouragement?

Who can support you by offering wisdom/guidance?

Who can support you by providing access to resources you'll need?

Who can support you by combining efforts with you to magnify the impact of your giving?

Invite these individuals to be part of your Giving Mastermind, and write those who agree to join in the "Giving Mastermind" section below. Note that you can have more or less than 10 individuals in your mastermind; add lines if needed. Realize that you will need to offer them support in their efforts as well.

Giving Mastermind

1. _____

2. _____

3. _____

4. _____

5. _____

6. _____

7. _____

8. _____

9. _____

10. _____

6. Dedicate time each week to journaling about how you feel after you donate your money, time, and talent. At the end of each month, record some of the highlights below.

_____

_____

_____

_____

_____

_____

_____

_____

_____

_____

_____

_____

_____

_____

_____

_____

_____

_____

7. Once you have reached your ultimate giving goal, record the occasion below.

    How do you feel? What has the experience been like? Are there any news clippings or mementos related to the occasion that you can replicate or attach below? How can you build on this gift from here?

_____

_____

NOTES

1. Napoleon Hill, *Grow Rich! with Peace of Mind* (New York, NY: Fawcett Columbine, 1967), vi–vi.

2. Ibid., 67–68.

3. Ibid., 68.

4. Ibid., vi.

5. Ibid., 45.

6. Napoleon Hill, *The Master-Key to Riches* (Shippensburg, PA: Sound Wisdom, 2018), 240.

7. Napoleon Hill, *Think and Grow Rich* (Shippensburg, PA: Sound Wisdom, 2017), 58.

8. Hill, *Grow Rich!*, 89.

9. Ibid., 19.

10. Hill qtd. in Jim Stovall, *Top of the Hill: Learning to Think and Grow Rich at Napoleon Hill High School* (Shippensburg, PA: Sound Wisdom, 2017), 61.

11. Hill, *Grow Rich!*, 73.

12. David Williams, "A Frugal Social Worker Left $11 Million to Children's Charities in His Will," CNN.com, last updated December 29, 2018, http://www.cnn.com/2018/12/28/us/frugal-social-worker-leaves-millions-to-charity-trnd/index.html.

13. Hill, *Grow Rich!*, 61.

14. Jim Stovall, *The Ultimate Gift* (Colorado Springs, CO: RiverOak, 2001), 112.

15. Napoleon Hill, "Master Mind: The Memoirs of Napoleon Hill," digital reproduction of the original manuscript, n.d., the Napoleon Hill Foundation, 71.

16. Ibid.

17. "*Think and Grow Rich* Reviews," SoundWisdom.com, 2019, http://www.soundwisdom.com/think-and-grow-rich-reviews.

18. Bryan Cronan, "How Chick-Fil-A's S. Truett Cathy Pioneered the Charitable Business," *The Christian Science Monitor*, September 8, 2014, http://www.csmonitor.com/Business/2014/0908/How-Chick-Fil-A-s-S.-Truett-Cathy-pioneered-the-charitable-business.

19. Ibid.

20. Steven A. Morelli, "What Tremendous Means Today," InsuranceNewsNet.com, Inc., August 14, 2017, http://insurancenewsnet.com/sponsor/tremendous-means-today#.XklcjhNKhTZ.

21. Steve Forbes, "How Billionaires Are Fixing Philanthropy," *The Washington Post*, June 16, 2014, http://www.washingtonpost.com/posteverything/wp/2014/06/16/thank-the-rich-for-supporting-the-underclass.

22. Hill, *Grow Rich!*, 27.

23. Ibid., 44.
24. Hill, "Master Mind," 274.
25. Ibid.
26. Hill, *Grow Rich!*, 62.
27. Hill, *Grow Rich!*, 77–89.
28. "Remembering George Herbert: 10 Quotes from the Great Priest and Poet," *Christian Today*, February 27, 2017, http://www.christiantoday.com/article/remembering-george-herbert-10-quotes-from-the-great-priest-and-poet/105062.htm.

ABOUT THE AUTHORS

Jim Stovall

In spite of his blindness, Jim Stovall has been a National Olympic weightlifting champion, a successful investment broker, the president of the Emmy Award-winning Narrative Television Network, and a highly sought-after author and platform speaker. He is the author of 40 books, including the bestseller *The Ultimate Gift*, which is now a major motion picture from 20th Century Fox starring James Garner and Abigail Breslin. Eight of his other novels have also been made into movies, with two more in production.

Steve Forbes, president and CEO of *Forbes* magazine, says, "Jim Stovall is one of the most extraordinary men of our era."

For his work in making television accessible to our nations 13 million blind and visually impaired people, The President's Committee on Equal Opportunity selected him as the Entrepreneur of the Year. Jim Stovall has been featured in *The Wall Street Journal*, *Forbes*, *USA Today*, and has been seen on *Good Morning America*, *CNN*, and *CBS Evening News*. He was also chosen as the International Humanitarian of the Year, joining

Jimmy Carter, Nancy Reagan, and Mother Teresa as recipients of this honor.

Jim Stovall can be reached at 918-627-1000 or Jim@JimStovall.com

Don Green

A resident of Wise, Virginia, the birthplace of Napoleon Hill, Don Green brings nearly 45 years of banking, finance, and entrepreneurship experience to his role as Executive Director of the Napoleon Hill Foundation. His first youthful business venture was charging admission to see his pet bear—yes, the living, growling kind! Since 2000, Green has traveled worldwide and used his finance skills to grow the Foundation's funds in order to continue the Foundation's educational outreach. Green has both modeled leadership skills as a CEO and taught them through the PMA Science of Success course at the University of Virginia's College at Wise. Don specializes in discussing his personal experiences in leadership and providing audiences with proven methods of applying Dr. Hill's success philosophy to business.